THE TAJ MAHAL AT AGRA, INDIA, HAS BEEN CALLED THE
MOST PERFECT GEM OF ARCHITECTURE EVER CONSTRUCTED

MOVING MILLIONS

The Pageant of Modern India

GERTRUDE L. WARNER
BISHOP J. WASKOM PICKETT
ALICE B. VAN DOREN
BELLE CHONÉ OLIVER, M.D.
LYMAN B. CARRUTHERS, M.D.
C. HERBERT RICE
MARY C. RICE
THE RT. REV. V. S. AZARIAH
E. STANLEY JONES

INTRODUCTION BY ROBERT E. SPEER

BOSTON
THE CENTRAL COMMITTEE ON THE
UNITED STUDY OF FOREIGN MISSIONS
and
THE MISSIONARY EDUCATION MOVEMENT
OF THE UNITED STATES AND CANADA

COPYRIGHT 1938
BY THE CENTRAL COMMITTEE ON
THE UNITED STUDY OF FOREIGN MISSIONS
BOSTON, MASSACHUSETTS

PRINTED BY THE VERMONT PRINTING COMPANY, BRATTLEBORO
MANUFACTURED IN THE UNITED STATES OF AMERICA

I

GERTRUDE LEGGETT WARNER was born in Mississippi and the flavor of the southern pines is still in her racy speech. Educated along with Bishop Pickett and Stanley Jones at Asbury College, no one expected her to become a missionary. She seemed to be too much in love with life, its beauty and joy. But she found new joy and beauty when she married Dr. A. N. Warner and went with him to India as a "girl bride" at the age of eighteen. For twenty-eight years they have filled various places in the Marathi field of the Methodist Episcopal Church. While mothering four delightful children, she has kept close to the soul of India through intuitive sympathy and through study of contemporaneous events in these stirring years.

II

BISHOP J. WASKOM PICKETT is the authority on mass movements. He began his missionary work in India as pastor and district superintendent in areas where these movements were taking place. In 1928 the National Christian Council, with the assistance of the Institute of Social and Religious Research of New York, initiated a comprehensive and thorough study of mission work in selected sections of the country where people had become Christians in groups and by the hundreds. Dr. Pickett was chosen as the director of the research, and his book *Christian Mass Movements in India* is a report of that study. In 1936 he was elected Bishop by the Central Conference of the Methodist Episcopal Church of Southern Asia, and assigned to the Bombay area.

III

ALICE BOUCHER VAN DOREN graduated in 1903 from Mt. Holyoke College, and in October of the same year sailed for India. Her graduate work in education was done at Teachers College, Columbia University, during furloughs. Her first two terms in India were spent in educational work under the Reformed Church in America in Ranipettai, South India. During her third and fourth terms she served as acting principal of St. Christopher Training College, Madras, in whose support eleven missionary boards are now cooperating, and spent several years as principal of the Sherman School in Chittoor. Seven years spent as educational secretary of the National Christian Council, gave wide opportunities for travel in India, Burma and Ceylon. Miss Van Doren has written, edited and contributed to a number of books, among them two published by the Central Committee on the United Study of Foreign Missions—*Lighted to Lighten* and *Christ Comes to the Village*.

IV

BELLE CHONÉ OLIVER, M.D., graduated in medicine in 1900 from the University of Toronto and, after an internship in the Women's Hospital, Philadelphia, she went to India under the Foreign Mission Board of what is now the United Church of Canada. During her first two terms she served in different stations, and in 1915 was sent to open up medical work in Benswara, S. Rajputana, where the mission began work among the aboriginals, the Bhils. After serving in various capacities that gave her personal knowledge of medical work in India, and attending the Jerusalem Conference

3

as a delegate, she became in 1933 the first full time secretary of the Christian Medical Association of India.

LYMAN B. CARRUTHERS, M.D., is a Canadian by birth and education. After serving for two years on the faculty of Cornell University, he was appointed a medical missionary to India under the Presbyterian Board in the U. S. A. He is Dean of the medical school at Miraj in the Bombay Presidency. He and his associates take great pride in the record of the young Indian doctors, many of them from low-caste families, who have gone out from this school.

V

REV. C. HERBERT RICE, D.D., is a graduate of Wooster College, Ohio, and Auburn Theological Seminary. He was for twenty-three years connected with Forman Christian College, Lahore. He is now principal of Allahabad Christian College, a Presbyterian institution for young men and boys, including Ewing Christian College, University College, the Allahabad Agricultural Institute and Jumna High School.

MRS. MARY COMPTON RICE is also a graduate of Wooster College and has been in India since 1913. One of her special interests is a great class of eighty men, women and children most of whom belong to the "Depressed Classes." This class, which crowds her home and verandas every Sunday, is an amazing demonstration of the dramatic movement taking place today amongst these people.

VI

THE RT. REV. V. S. AZARIAH, BISHOP OF DORNAKAL, is the son of a Hindu Untouchable who was converted to Christianity and became a clergyman. The well educated son worked for thirteen years as South India secretary of the Y. M. C. A. and later offered himself for direct missionary work in the wilderness of Dornakal. The English Church deciding to install an Indian bishop, Dr. Azariah was consecrated first Bishop of Dornakal on December 29th, 1912, in St. Paul's Cathedral, Calcutta. During the early days in Dornakal he lived in a tent, and later he and his wife brought up their family in a two room cottage. Bishop Azariah has traveled extensively in India, Australia, New Zealand, Europe and America. The University of Cambridge conferred on him the degree of LL.D. Honoris Causa.

VII

REV. E. STANLEY JONES, D.D., first served in India as pastor and District Superintendent in the Methodist Episcopal Mission. He was called into a wider field of service as evangelist to the educated and student classes of the land. Following this he accepted invitations to take the message to the United States, South America, Europe, Africa and China, until now his dynamic Christ-centered personality is known around the world. The books which he has written also reveal that vital divine touch so characteristic of his message. During the summer holidays he conducts an Ashram in the Himalaya Mountains where representatives of all groups and classes of people gather for refreshment of body, mind and spirit.

CONTENTS

	PAGE
BIOGRAPHIES OF AUTHORS	3
LIST OF ILLUSTRATIONS	9
INTRODUCTION	10
POEM—WITH OPEN HEART	12

CHAPTER ONE
THE MIRACLE OF MODERN INDIA

GEORGE V ENTERS THE GATEWAY	13
TWENTY-SIX YEARS LATER	15
INDIA BECOMING A NATION	19
THE PERIOD OF GREATEST BRITISH INFLUENCE	20
AGITATION FOR SELF-GOVERNMENT	22
CONFLICTING VIEWPOINTS	24
THE INDIAN NATIONAL CONGRESS	25
THE NEW CONSTITUTION	27
OUTSTANDING LEADERS	29
INDIAN WOMEN IN THE NEW DAY	32
PEACEFUL PICKETING	35
INFLUENTIAL WOMEN	36
GREAT RELIGIOUS PROBLEMS	39

CHAPTER TWO
THE UNTOUCHABLES

WHY "UNTOUCHABLES"?	43
WHAT IT MEANS TO BE AN UNTOUCHABLE	44
THE ORIGINS OF UNTOUCHABILITY	45
EFFECT OF OCCUPATIONAL RESTRICTIONS	47
NOT DISTINGUISHED BY DIRT, STUPIDITY OR VICE	48
SOME CHARACTERISTICS OF UNTOUCHABLES	49
NUMBERS AND LOCATION	51
THE HINDU RELIGION AND UNTOUCHABILITY	53
REVOLTS	55
MISSIONARY POLICY	57
GROUP RESPONSE	58
THE POWER OF PREACHING	59
TRANSFORMATION OF UNTOUCHABLES	60
ASSETS OF THE NATION	61
THE GROWTH OF CHRISTIAN MASS MOVEMENTS	62
MR. GANDHI AND CHRISTIAN CONVERSION	64

	PAGE
THE EMERGENCE OF DR. AMBEDKAR	66
DISILLUSIONMENT	67
THE FIGHT FOR A SHARE IN LAW-MAKING	69
AN EXPERIENCE WITH PRAYER	70
RELIGION CONDEMNED AND RELIGION REQUIRED	70
SOULS FOR AUCTION?	71
THE GREAT DECISION	72
THE CHRISTIAN PROSPECT	73

CHAPTER THREE
INDIA'S RURAL MILLIONS

DRASTIC CHANGES IN VILLAGE LIFE	77
LEADERS OF CHANGING CONDITIONS	78
NEEDS OF VILLAGE LIFE: LITERACY	81
VILLAGE SCHOOLS	83
ADULT EDUCATION	85
SANITATION AND HEALTH	88
ECONOMIC UPLIFT	89
AGRICULTURAL SCHOOLS	90
COTTAGE INDUSTRIES	92
COOPERATIVE MARKETING	93
AN INDIAN CHRISTIAN VILLAGE	94
UPLIFT OF RURAL WOMEN	96
THE NEED OF CHRISTIAN FAITH	97
STRIKING RESULTS IN LEADERSHIP	99

CHAPTER FOUR
THE MINISTRY OF HEALING IN INDIA

THE SCUDDER MEMORIAL HOSPITAL	102
EARLY WOMEN DOCTORS	104
MEDICAL COMPETITION: AMERICA OR INDIA?	105
GOVERNMENTAL AGENCIES	107
WIDE-SPREAD MEDICAL MISSIONS	109
ZENANA HOSPITALS	111
EVANGELISTIC WORK IN HOSPITALS	113
HIGHER HEALTH STANDARDS	114
THE LEPERS OF INDIA	115
TREATMENT OF TUBERCULOSIS	118
MEDICAL PIONEERING	119
PUBLIC HEALTH CAMPAIGNS	120
THE NURSING PROFESSION	122
THE NEED FOR ADEQUATE MEDICAL TRAINING	123
INDIAN CHRISTIAN DOCTORS	127
RESPONSIBILITY OF MEDICAL MISSIONS	128
WIDE OPPORTUNITIES	129

CHAPTER FIVE
HIGHER CHRISTIAN EDUCATION IN INDIA

	PAGE
CHRISTIAN MISSIONS AND EDUCATIONAL PIONEERING	131
BEGINNINGS OF AN EDUCATIONAL SYSTEM	133
EDUCATIONAL PIONEERS	134
HIGHER CHRISTIAN EDUCATION IN INDIA TODAY	135
INDIAN EDUCATIONAL LEADERSHIP	136
HIGHER CHRISTIAN EDUCATION FOR WOMEN	138
NEW EMPHASIS ON EDUCATION FOR GIRLS	140
EXAMPLES OF CHRISTIAN COLLEGES FOR WOMEN	141
IMPORTANCE OF WOMEN'S COLLEGES	145
COEDUCATION	146
PROMINENT WOMEN	147
SPECIAL PROBLEMS IN CHRISTIAN HIGHER EDUCATION	149
THE LINDSAY COMMISSION	149
THE INFLUENCE OF CHRISTIAN INSTITUTIONS	151
CENTERS OF CHRISTIAN LIFE AND SERVICE	154
DESIRE FOR CHRISTIAN UNITY	156
THE STUDENT CHRISTIAN MOVEMENT	157
WHY MAINTAIN CHRISTIAN COLLEGES IN INDIA?	159
A STATESMAN'S ESTIMATE	161

CHAPTER SIX
THE CHRISTIAN CHURCH IN INDIA

A VILLAGE CHURCH	165
STAGES OF MISSIONARY WORK	167
THE INDIAN CHURCH DEFINED	170
ORGANIZATION	174
ECCLESIASTICAL ORGANIZATIONS	176
INDIAN LEADERSHIP	178
THE CHURCH IN INDIAN CIVIC LIFE	180
CHRISTIAN LITERACY	181
CHRISTIAN GIVING	182
MOVEMENTS TOWARDS UNITY	185
FELLOWSHIP AND COOPERATION	188
SPIRITUAL LIFE AND WITNESS-BEARING	189
MISSIONARY WORK OF THE INDIAN CHURCH	192

CHAPTER SEVEN
FACING THE FUTURE TASK

THE CHRISTIAN APPROACH TO INDIA	196
THE MISSIONARY APPROACH TO THE WEST	209
STATISTICAL TABLES	217
BIBLIOGRAPHY	219
INDEX	223

LIST OF ILLUSTRATIONS

FACING
PAGE

The Taj Mahal at Agra, India, Has Been Called the Most Perfect Gem of Architecture Ever Constructed................*Frontispiece*

A Procession of a Maharaja in India........................... 16

Women Picket Bombay Council Elections...................... 17

Typical Outcaste Section of an Indian Village.................. 64

A Sunday School for Non-Christian Children in Tanners Village, Nipani 65

Modern Methods of Ploughing. Agricultural Institute, Allahabad, India 80

Sangli Movable School—All Loaded........................... 81

Patients Arriving at the Hospital, Kasganj, India............... 128

The General Ward (interior) the Union Mission Tuberculosis Sanitorium, Arogyavarum, in South India...................... 129

The Student Body on the Campus of the Lucknow Christian College, India 144

In the Booksellers' Bazaar, Lucknow.......................... 145

The Right Reverend V. S. Azariah, D.D., Bishop of Dornakal.... 192

Village Worship Platform at Arthala, Ghazeabad District........ 193

Dr. E. Stanley Jones with Two Nationalist Leaders Who Are Wearing the Gandhi Cap....................................... 208

All Saints' Memorial Church, Peshawar........................ 209

8

INTRODUCTION

NOWHERE else in condensed and yet adequate form can any such account of present day India be found as is presented in this little book. The writers are all sympathetic friends of India, loving India so much that they are giving their lives to her service. They know the conditions of which they write and they set forth in an absolutely trustworthy way the present situation of India's more than three hundred million people. Their account of the political situation is more hopeful than it could have been one or two years ago. And the stir among the Untouchables and the steady growth of the Church give evidence of the greatness of the missionary opportunity.

Indeed the door of opportunity for Christianity never was more open in India in the past and it is more open than in any other land in the world today. There is no abridgement of religious liberty by law. The caste system, social pressure, the communal system of elections, the constraint of religious traditionalism and economic conditions hamper a free response to the appeal of the Gospel, but these moral and social hindrances cannot invoke any legal prohibition to the free preaching of Christianity and to its free acceptance. It is clear, moreover, that these millions are in reality moving. Already the profoundest changes have taken place. The deepest and greatest of all changes is yet to take place in India's acceptance of Christ.

Long ago the voice of Keshab Chunder Sen of the Brahmo Samaj proclaimed what would some day occur. When in 1879 he delivered his address on "Who is Christ?" he declared that India was "destined to become Christian" and "could not escape her destiny." And then he added, "Gentlemen, you cannot deny that your hearts have been touched, conquered and subjugated by a higher power. That power, need I tell you, is Christ. It is Christ who rules British India, not the British government. None but Jesus, none but Jesus, none but Jesus ever dreamed this bright, this precious diadem, India, and Jesus shall have it."

Contemporary voices are saying as much. A modern leader of the Brahmo Samaj declares, "There is no one else seriously bidding for the heart of the world except Jesus Christ. There is no one else on the field."

May the study of this book not only give to its readers a reliable and sympathetic picture of the India of today but may it also lead many of them to give their lives to India's evangelization and Christian service.

—ROBERT E. SPEER.

MOVING MILLIONS

WITH OPEN HEART

Freedom! Freedom! Freedom!
To the Pariahs, to the Tiyas, to the Pulayas,[1] Freedom!
To the Paravas, to the Kuravas, to the Maravas, Freedom!

> Come let us labour, all,
> Sparing naught and hurting none,
> Walking in the way of truth and light.
>
> There shall be none of low degree,
> And none shall be oppressed.
> Born in India all are of noble birth.
> Wealth and learning may they flourish
> With joy of mind! Let us live
> Like brothers all alike.
>
> Perish ignorance
> In man and woman alike!
> No more subordination,
> In every walk of life, equality!
> Man and woman shall equal be
> In this land of ours.

Freedom! Freedom! Freedom!
To the Pariahs, to the Tiyas, to the Pulayas, Freedom!
To the Paravas, the Kuravas, to the Maravas, Freedom!

—SUBRAHAMANYAM BHARATI.
Translated from the Tamil.

[1] Names of particular castes low down in the social scale.

CHAPTER I

THE MIRACLE OF MODERN INDIA

By GERTRUDE L. WARNER

BOMBAY the beautiful!" The wonderful natural harbor is generously dotted with picturesque islands. Innumerable ships laden with the produce and odors of Colombo, Hongkong, Shanghai, Kobe, Liverpool, New York, Amsterdam, Sydney, San Francisco, yes, of the whole world, are handling cargo at her great modern docks. Her shore is edged with buildings of architectural beauty.

GEORGE V ENTERS THE GATEWAY

Stand with me, and let us consider the miracle of modern India as we look back to December 2, 1911, when as a very young and enthusiastic missionary I stood overlooking this gateway of India.

A cloudless sky; the sea, rippled with laughter by the slightest of breezes, glistens, sparkles and dances with the glee of festive preparations, for King George V and Queen Mary, as the first reigning British sovereigns ever to visit India, are landing on our shores today to be proclaimed Emperor and Empress of India.

What splendor! What pageantry! It would be difficult to decide which people more truly love or more ably present dignified and impressive pageantry—the English or the Indian. Combine the two and you have the most colorful processions and ceremonies that this world has ever seen.

Throughout the city great arches, representative of the history of the people and their industries, have been constructed. Through the generosity particularly of the wealthier Parsee citizens, aided by the animated spirit and help of the entire population, funds have been raised for the elaborate decoration and illumination of the city. As we look from our vantage point, we see a pavilion constructed in the Saracenic style, dazzling white, temporarily erected for the reception of their Majesties.

Many of the notables of India are assembled. Central among them is His Excellency the Viceroy, second only in his exalted position to the King-Emperor himself. We see also the Governor of Bombay, his bodyguard resplendent in scarlet and gold; officers of the royal Indian navy and the royal Indian marine in their smartest uniforms; the highest officials of the civil and military régime; the diplomatic representatives of the world in their varied and brilliant uniforms. The English police force are on duty wearing their white helmets and starched white uniforms into which it looks as if they themselves had been starched and ironed. Their Indian associates, in their blue and yellow uniforms, are no less impressive.

Far more imposing and picturesque is that large group representative of the aristocracy and intelligentsia of India: wealthy Parsees and Brahmans from the various provinces representative of the great Hindu India. Influential Mohammedans, Jews, Sikhs and Christians are generously enough sprinkled throughout the crowd to emphasize these strong influential minorities which are destined to play such an important part in the maze of Indian politics.

The Indian ladies from the different religious groups, each attired after the fashion of the area from which she comes, and their men folk in their turbans and varied headdress of rich royal colors, add a rainbow touch and charm to the occasion. A handsome Rajput prince with his colorful suite reminds us of that large section of Indian royalty that have already assembled with their picturesque retinues in Delhi, where they will pass in brilliant procession before their Majesties.

Twenty-six Years Later

Let us view another important historic event in Bombay in the year 1937, with a new King-Emperor on the throne, George VI, and try to sense the tremendous changes that have come to India in the intervening years. On his coronation day on May 12, 1937, we sit in the drawing room of a friend and hear distinctly over the radio the entire coronation service. We hold in our hands a printed copy of the service as it is taking place in London and follow it during the broadcast—the first time in the history of the British Empire that a king on his coronation day has addressed his people directly. His voice is heard in the homes of the lowly and the rich, throughout not only the British Empire, but the world.

Again Bombay becomes an enchanted island. The brilliant electric illuminations outlining in artistic designs the magnificent Government and private buildings in red, white and blue, turn the city into a veritable fairyland. We join with hundreds of thousands in a procession following the same route as that royal procession of December 2, 1911, through this cosmopolitan city which in miniature is so illustrative of the growing unity of India.

The procession wends its way first through the modern city of up-to-date hotels, apartment houses, smart English shops, banks and offices. Leaving the broad roads of the Fort we plunge into the Indian city, where India's varied peoples daily rub shoulders. The hum of business is stilled but the busy, moving and gesticulating crowds in gala holiday garb fill the streets. At intervals the blue-uniformed, yellow-turbaned police, drawn largely from the local Hindu population, stand on duty. The many-tinted houses with gay new coats of color-washing of yellow, white and red; the luxurious carvings on the pillars of wood; the balconies overhanging the streets, crowded with people; the rosettes of windows, all lend to the effectiveness of the picture. This is the center of the Hindu commercial community.

A PROCESSION OF A MAHARAJA IN INDIA

WOMEN PICKET BOMBAY COUNCIL ELECTIONS

Ewing Galloway, N. Y.

As the procession wends its way, proud Maratha people, residents of this area, who altogether number sixteen millions and were the last to give allegiance to the
British Raj, gaze from their shops and houses. No doubt
many of them are remembering the important part their
people played in making India's history and are dream-
ing of what they will contribute to the new India, proud
in the thought that from the very beginning of the present struggle for independence, leaders from their group
have been in the forefront.

The Gujaratis, keen men in business and politics, the
group to which Mr. Gandhi belongs, also watch and
march in this procession. They are justly proud of what
their eight million people have contributed to this miracle of India.

A group of Tamil people—the men with long tufts
of hair done on the tops of their heads, their women
folk dressed in highly colored saris, yellow and red pre-
dominating—are silently gazing and thinking of the millions in their Tamil land of the south with its own
peculiar culture. They are secretly wondering just how
truly their Tamil traditions are going to survive in this
all-absorbing nation-forming process. A glimpse into the
crowd reveals many of their neighbors, the Telugus of
the southeast coast, whose extensive Andhra-land has
been divided up, during these years of building a new
India, among different states and the Madras Presidency.

Proud, sensitive, and bare-headed Bengalis stand by,

no doubt at this moment filled with passionate devotion to mother Bengal. The Biharis, the few who have come to this great inviting commercial city for work or trade, gaze on the procession but have not forgotten their rich traditions, though far from their homes. Punjabis, Oriyas, groups of proud, handsome Rajputs, Kanarese and Malayalis elbowing their way in the crowd, represent their millions of home folk hundreds of miles from this scene. All this mixture of tongues, races and religions is the visible result of invasions in centuries long past. Each of these awakening people has its own "native land" within this great sub-continent, its own language, its own customs, and its own literature. Each has alphabets and modes of writing, different from the others. We have had a kaleidoscopic view of the varied races who make up Hindu India.

Leaving this part of Bombay, the procession passes through Bhendi Bazaar, the center of the Moslem community, representative of more than seventy-seven million of India's population. They are an important part of the world community that follows this faith. Since many of them are under British rule, any crisis among them in Turkey, Arabia, Palestine or Africa affects the situation in India and vice-versa. Britain is often accused of showing partiality to this minority group in order to make safer her world position. Every section of this community is to be seen in the streets or gazing from the tops of the houses as the procession advances.

We note particularly that the tall stalwart hill-men, the Afghans and the Baluchis, who have still the hardy look of the mountains, are sharing the enthusiasm of the occasion with their co-religionists. At latticed windows, and from the curtained windows of modern motor cars, veiled Moslem ladies peep shyly on the scenes about them. They are a reminder of the millions of women of India who still observe this most unhealthful custom of *purdah*.

India Becoming a Nation

In leaving this procession let us visualize the divided India of the centuries now approaching the possibility of working as a nation. Is this the India which is the mother of at least four of the world's living religions, Hinduism, Buddhism, Jainism and Sikhism? Yes, this is the India which is also the result of successive invasions that have poured down upon her through the mountain passes in the extreme northwest. Here is epitomized the India which has been overrun by Indo-Europeans, Scythians, Huns, Afghans, Persians, Mongols and Turks. Yes, this is the same India also whose later invaders have come to her from the sea—the Europeans, Portuguese, Dutch, Danes, French and English —seamen all.

When George VI came to the throne, he looked upon a vastly different political India from that over which his father began to reign some twenty-six years earlier. In this period there arose that fervent national spirit which has done more to unite all India into one people speaking one voice, than any other fact in her history. As our children's children read Indian history, time lending to it a more correct perspective, they will say, "Surely the welding of this great sub-continent into the nation we know as the India of our day is a miracle of the first magnitude in nation building."

The Period of Greatest British Influence

Just eighty years ago India came directly under the English Crown. Railway travel increased in volume and popularity by leaps and bounds. Factories and modern industrialism began to appear in larger cities. There was an abnormal enthusiasm for English education and the high schools and colleges were insufficient to meet the pressing demands. Sons of wealthier high caste parents, by hundreds and thousands, defied Hindu prejudice and crossed the "black water" to England and America to complete their English education. This was the period when India was most under the control of the West.

The Russo-Japanese War in 1905 was truly a landmark in human history, whose significance increases with the lapse of time. It sent a thrill throughout Asia to have little Japan, an Oriental nation, win a victory over a European Power. Educated young Indians everywhere began to ask, "Why cannot India become free and strong like Japan?" It is from this date that the control of the West and white dominance began to ebb. Many educated Indians began in real earnest their political agitation against British rule. The assassin's bomb and bullet came into use with almost a religious fervor.

Following this period of agitation, in 1909, Great Britain granted political concessions in the form of the Morley-Minto Reforms. They made no breach with the old system. While they extended the sphere of popular influence, the controlling power remained in London. Thus there continued the rising tide of dissatisfaction, almost despair, in the minds of political Indian leaders. However, there remained in the masses a strong confidence in British good will and justice, as was so very strikingly evident in the hour of Britain's greatest need, the World War. India rallied to the aid of her foreign King-Emperor with a million and a quarter of her picked young men. She sent to the front one hundred thousand more soldiers than Australia, New Zealand and Canada combined. She sent from her supplies also the tracks, rolling stock, engines, coal, and staff for the strategic railways in Mesopotamia. This service was rendered by all classes, rich and poor alike. The princes of India were generous contributors; while out of the poverty of the great masses of the people she gave a billion dollars in gifts and war loans, truly an epic of sacrifice. She did this with the increasing hope that, with an Allied victory, Britain would demonstrate her larger confidence in India's people by placing more of the country's affairs in their hands.

AGITATION FOR SELF-GOVERNMENT

On August 20, 1917, the Secretary of State for India, the Right Honorable Edwin Montagu, expressing no doubt the deep gratitude of the British Empire to India, gave her this solemn promise: "The policy of His Majesty's Government, with which the Government of India are in complete accord, is that of the increasing association of Indians in every branch of the administration and the gradual development of self-governing institutions with a view to the progressive realization of responsible government in India as an integral part of the British Empire. . . . ." This declaration was followed by an act of Parliament in 1919 known as the Montagu-Chelmsford Reforms. These constitutional changes, which would have been hailed even five years previously as epoch-making, were unhesitatingly denounced on their appearance as overdue, incomplete, disappointing and unsatisfactory. The Home Rule movement had grown rapidly during the war, and thus self-government was now immediately demanded by the extremist group as their reward for loyalty. The days became increasingly difficult. Hate and misunderstanding took the place of calm, balanced judgment. The pace of constitutional advance seemed unthinkably slow to the extremist groups, the progress in nation-building almost imperceptible.

The Montagu-Chelmsford Act held two definite aims in view.

In the British provinces in India, which now number eleven, the aim was to set up in each a unit of the new constitutional democracy. In the provincial governments, the clumsy system called dyarchy, that is the system of dividing responsibility between British and Indians, was to be followed. The departments of revenue, justice, irrigation, police, and prisons were held by the British. The departments of agriculture, industry, local self-government, public works, health, education, and excise were transferred to the Indian ministers. The ministers were responsible to the legislatures and were elected on the basis that each Indian religious community should have its share of numbers proportionate to its size and influence. Thus we have the communal system, which becomes such a vital political issue to the Hindu when millions of their numbers, the Untouchables, threaten to leave the Hindu community to join some other religious community.

The second purpose of the reforms was to increase decidedly the Indian element in the Central Government, at Delhi. The aim here was additional representation which would increase the membership of Indians in the Viceroy's Executive Council, his cabinet. The Central Government, which is made up of the Council of State and the Legislative Assembly, had important powers. They voted supplies, made laws, criticized and even censured the administration. But the one thing that remained constantly the red flag to the Indian Nationalist was that the power of veto continued to rest in the British Viceroy's hands.

CONFLICTING VIEWPOINTS

It would be impossible in such a brief review to mention all the important political events that crowded one upon another following the adoption of these reforms. From 1919 on, the atmosphere became increasingly inflamed. Plainly there were two conflicting viewpoints which must be reconciled: that of the British, who remained the controlling power granting concessions; and that of the Indian Nationalists, who claimed the full right to control affairs in their own country. It was recognized that only full knowledge, mutual understanding, and a sympathetic attitude for the good of both in cooperative service could offer hope of reconciling these conflicting purposes.

At length in 1928 the Simon Commission was first sent to India to study the situation and to secure the facts on which a revised plan of government would be framed. It secured them in the face of intense opposition and boycott. We can well understand why. It was without Indian representation.

So again came the Simon Commission a few months later. This time it added Indian personnel. Following this were the Round Table Conferences in London in

1930, 1931, and 1932, with the purpose of including the widest possible Indian representation. At one of these conferences Mr. Gandhi was present as the sole representative of the Indian National Congress. But the conflicting viewpoints remained so distinct that he returned to his native land only again to share the fate of imprisonment with thousands of his fellow citizens.

However, while Government continued to hold a strong hand on radical Nationalist activities, there were liberal minds both British and Indian, hammering away on the new India Constitution. It was necessarily a slow process. To quote from J. A. Spender, "There are no analogies which exactly fit the case of India; in the long run she must find her own solutions, but a recognition of the essential differences between the Government of a homogeneous country like Great Britain and that of a continent like India, is in this respect the beginning of wisdom."[1] It is indeed a new thing in history that is being attempted.

THE INDIAN NATIONAL CONGRESS

India has gradually developed an increasingly effective organization through which to express her aspirations, the Indian National Congress. The intelligentsia had as early as 1885, with seventy-two delegates from the various provinces of India, met together with a group of

[1] J. A. Spender, *Great Britain, Empire and Commonwealth*, p. 758. London, Cassell & Co., 1936.

sympathetic Englishmen, to establish the Indian National
Congress. The language of this first conference was mild
and complimentary, but in later years it became caustic
and critical. This change of attitude has been most significant, for it has more certainly sensed and more effectively expressed the rising tide of Nationalism than
either the Hindu Mahasabha, which represents the orthodox conservative Hindu group, or the All-India Moslem
League, which represents Moslem opinion. The Congress is an all-Indian organization and meets each au-
tumn or winter during some all-Indian holiday season,
each time in a different part of the country, that its en-
thusiasms and ideas may be more widely diffused.

The high-water mark of Congress achievement thus
far reached was in the elections of 1937, when thirty-five
million cast their vote for representation under the
new constitution with its unprecedented extension of
franchise. Their candidates gained the majority in six
provinces out of eleven. With the tacit control of these
six provincial governments in their hands, for four
months they continued to defer taking office, vigorously
contesting the right of British veto. However, as this is
being written, in late July, 1937, they have reached an
agreement to accept their posts, and the elected delegates are taking their places in the Provincial Councils
and Central Assembly. Meanwhile, Mr. Gandhi is telling
the world, "The office acceptance by the Congress in the
prosecution of its goal of complete independence, is a

serious attempt, on the one hand, to avoid a bloody revolution and on the other hand to avoid more civil disobedience on a scale hitherto never attempted."

Undoubtedly Great Britain has been an outstanding contributor to the national unity of India. The fact that this world power is transferring the reins of Government in an orderly constitutional way, without revolution, will forever be to her credit and also to the credit of India's people, who have so strikingly proved to the world that there are ways to obtain rights without revolution.

THE NEW CONSTITUTION

April 1, 1937, will go on record as an historic date for India, as it marks the time when the first section of the new constitution came into force. The constitution of the United States of America can be reproduced in some twenty printed pages, whereas in its effort to meet the perplexities of the situation, the Indian constitution covers over two hundred, with more than a hundred pages of schedules. Not only was the diversification of British India to be provided for, but as the Secretary of State for India, the Marquis of Zetland, rightly observes, "Perhaps the main element of complexity was the necessity of finding means whereby the Indian Princes, to whom one-fourth of the population of India owes allegiance, might be enabled for the first time, while preserving for the domestic affairs of their States their own forms of personal government, to unite their territories with British India as a single federation capable of administering the common concerns alike of Indian States and British Indian Provinces."[1]

The intensity of the perplexity is still more evident when we remember that there are some seven hundred of these Indian rajahs, great and small, ruling over one-third of the territory of India, from which the Nationalist propaganda has been persistently excluded. They are the best protected autocrats in the world, each with his direct relationship to the British Crown. Amongst them are some able, progressive and conscientious rulers. Of these might be mentioned the Maharajah of Mysore, well known for his interest in civic improvement, industrial advance, and scientific research; the Nizam of Hyderabad, whose capital is the fourth largest city of India, the progressive center of an area of 82,672 square miles, as large as England and Scotland, with a population of twelve and a half millions; and the Gaekwar of Baroda, who is working for the promotion of compulsory primary education and circulating libraries, as well as experiments in agriculture. This ruler visited America some years ago with the Maharani and brought back with him many new ideas. The state of Travancore is famous for its high degree of literacy, and the young Maharajah has

[1] Marquis of Zetland, "India's New Constitution," *Christian Science Monitor*, March 17, 1937.

stepped out into the limelight through his recent edict admitting Untouchables into orthodox Hindu temples. However, the great majority of these rajahs have but petty states and many of them continue to live the life of the Oriental despot.

OUTSTANDING LEADERS

Every great movement of history brings to the front certain outstanding characters. This is strikingly true of India, which has many reasons to be proud of her patriots who have so fearlessly and bravely served her during this period of transition.

Mohandas Karamchand Gandhi continues to be the figure that has captured the imagination of the world. It was he who for the first time in the history of India aroused the masses of this land to rally under one leader for one cause. How many times when his popularity has seemingly waned some people have said, "Gandhi is finished now. So far as politics go, we shall hear no more of him." Then as some new crisis has arisen his influence and reputation have again flashed like a meteor across the frontiers of the whole world. This insignificant looking man approaching his seventies, half ascetic, half shrewd scheming politician, remains an enigma even to his staunchest admirers and those working nearest to him.

Another Congress leader and man of charming personality is Jawaharlal Nehru. He is a handsome Kashmiri Brahman of wealth and social prominence who has captured the imagination of young India. He is India's eminent radical socialist patriot. He declares in no uncertain tones that before India can become the great nation she is capable of becoming, the Indian princes, the landowners, the capitalists and the *sadhus* (the Hindu mendicants) must go. The great question is, can his social program come into being without a bloody revolution? Because of his extreme views he has had to spend years in prison. His autobiography written while in prison and recently off the press is the most widely read political book in India and England today. He, as president of the Indian National Congress, during the last elections toured India by airplane, automobile, steamboat, canoe and bullock cart, on camels, on elephants and on foot, with the result that thirty-five million people cast their votes and Congress won by an overwhelming majority. Here is a dynamic character with whom undoubtedly India must reckon during the near future.

A group of men most valuable to India during these years of crisis and tension have been that fine, stalwart, brilliant and thoroughly devoted group of Liberals who so often have helped to keep the balance, and who so generously gave of themselves to help towards an understanding between the more radical national leaders and the government. On the one hand they refused to ally themselves with Civil Disobedience and the more radical Congress program, and on the other hand they sought to persuade the government to deal with the movement less harshly. In the end, they were able to act as mediators between the government and the imprisoned Congress leaders in bringing about the truce of 1930. Their wisdom and counsels of moderation were also of great value in the ensuing Round Table Conferences.

Leaders from the Moslem community have also made definite contributions as the miracle of modern India's social and political transformation has progressed.

Increasingly, Indian Christian leaders are registering influence in shaping India's future. This has not been so rapid as the varied and extensive penetration of the Christian leaven and the numerical growth of the Christian church would lead one naturally to expect. Among the many reasons for this are the facts that caste Hinduism has ostracized from family, social and political contact those who have dared to accept Christian baptism; that large numbers of the Christian community have come from the oppressed, poverty-stricken, illiterate masses; and also that the various reforms started by Christian backing and practice are, in part at least, being carried forward by other religious communities without formally accepting the Christ who actually initiated them. Added to these is the fact that those who have accepted the Christian faith are scattered throughout India, and their service, in Government, social re-

form, national advance, as doctors, teachers and in village uplift work, though massive in its total impact, is
not sufficiently spectacular to command social notoriety
or publicity.

INDIAN WOMEN IN THE NEW DAY

One of the most interesting and prophetic facts of this
new day in India is the increasing part women are taking
in Government as well as in social reforms. The Indian
National Congress is rightly encouraging this participation.

All true friends of India have raised their voices and
used their pens in trying to arouse public opinion with
regard to the centuries-old wrongs against Indian womanhood. Their battlecry has been, "Female education,
the remarriage of widows, and the raising of the age
of marriage." If we look only at statistics, we must admit that a pitifully small beginning has been made, even
after much consecrated, earnest effort. Yet at this very
point where during the past centuries the darkness has
been deepest and most impenetrable, today the light of
knowledge is penetrating, and we find the chief cause
for deep gratitude.

The All India Women's Conference, which held its
first session in 1926—with yearly sessions since—has already achieved unbelievable results. Among its outstanding achievements was the passing of the Sarda Act
in 1930. This act was framed by Mr. Harbilas Sarda. In

his bill he aimed to fix the minimum age of marriage for girls at fourteen years and for boys, eighteen years, and sought to decree that all marriages under that age be invalid. Had the law as he framed it been adopted it would certainly have created one of the greatest social revolutions of our day. This bill was debated for weeks and was finally passed, but in such an amended form that, in spite of all the work of the reformers and all the soul-agony of many of India's chief men and women, it was what leading Indian patriots disgustedly called "a dummy," a "dead thing," or "a law with all the teeth drawn." This, they pointed out, left the door open for child-marriages, for it permitted the performing of such marriages provided the parties involved paid a fine. Are not those of us who move among the people constantly being told, as we see marriage preparations, that they must now pay a "fee" to Government and is not that "fee" now added to the already crushingly heavy expense of marriage in India? As the Sarda Act stands to-day it is more educational than restrictive. Yet it has been a most noteworthy attempt to consolidate opinion favorable to this great social reform.

One of the richest experiences that has come to me in India was that of attending a session of the All India Women's Conference with Mrs. Sarojini Naidu, the famous Indian poetess, as president. It was challenging to witness these hundreds of women, Hindu, Mohammedan, Parsee, Christian and Theosophist, working side

by side for the good of the nation and for their sisters,
with never once a break, with no friction, and with no
"scenes."

On this occasion the late Lady Dorabji Tata, a Parsee,
gave an "At Home" to the Conference. Her home in
Bombay was a palace, one of the most magnificent
homes in the world. After elaborate refreshments we
were entertained by a great Russian-American pianist.
Mrs. Sarojini Naidu announced and interpreted his se-
lections. She is world famed as an eloquent orator. I have
attended many piano recitals in various parts of the
world but never one in such perfect surroundings: the
beautiful home, filled with hundreds of women of varied
religious beliefs in their beautiful costumes and their
exquisite jewelry.

However, the next morning as I looked from my
window out upon the squalor of our slums, and recalled
that, at most, only two women out of every hundred in
this fair land are literate, as I thought of child-marriage, enforced widowhood, *zenana* life, the *purdah*
system, and the opposition of the orthodox Hindu and
Mohammedan to every change, I realized that these
women, a mere drop from the vast ocean of India's
womanhood, had a difficult and perilous task ahead of
them. They are not blind to the fact that it may take
them generations to attain their goal, but they have put
their hands to the plough and they will never turn
back. These women have declared themselves as being

against caste distinctions, communal divisions, polygamy, *purdah,* child-marriage and sex discriminations. They have also declared themselves for equal rights of inheritance, and for free and compulsory education. Moreover they have plunged into the work to bring about these reforms. Mr. Gandhi knew what he was about when he called upon the women of India to follow him in his non-violent battle for freedom, nor did they disappoint him.

PEACEFUL PICKETING

During the tense days of 1931, when the non-violence campaign organized by Mr. Gandhi was in operation, many Indian society ladies of the various communities of Bombay discarded their dainty French slippers, and their imported Parisian silks, and donned the home-spun, home-woven *khaddar* worn by the Nationalist! And many of them counted it a privilege to go to jail to prove their genuine patriotism!

One night in Bombay when the rain poured as it can only pour during an Indian monsoon, a procession of Indian women from the best families in the city sat in the streets and open plazas, hour after hour, when their processions were stopped by the police. On another day of torrential rain, when the Bombay Legislative Assembly elections were to take place, the women went out by hundreds in that deluge because the Congress party had determined to boycott those elections; and so effective was their work that the elections were not held that day!

Can we forget the raid on the Dharsana Salt Works during the intense heat of May, 1930, when Sarojini Naidu was leading the procession and they were stopped by the police? It was then that she and her followers sat down in the dust of the road in the extreme heat, without water, and remained seated, hour after hour, spinning with their hand spindles, while they good-humoredly entertained each other and jokingly teased the police. It was a very common thing to see women, in saffron colored saris made of *khaddar,* sitting at the doors of liquor shops and where foreign cloth was being sold, doing what they called "peaceful picketing." Who will ever be able to estimate the influence they had?

INFLUENTIAL WOMEN

Dr. Muthulakshmi Reddy of Madras is a brilliant Hindu woman of outstanding ability who has taken an active part in politics, not with the Congress as Mrs. Naidu has done, but as a Liberal. She is known throughout India as a wise and competent legislator because of the splendid work she has so ably accomplished as a member of the Madras Legislative Assembly. When serving as president of the All India Women's Conference in Lahore, she said, "I feel that I would be failing in my duty if I did not offer a word of tribute to the several missionary organizations which have been the pioneers in the cause of female education. The women population of this country has been placed under a deep debt of gratitude to the several missionary agencies for their most valuable contributions to the educational uplift of the Indian women."

Later when discussing medical help for the women of India, she said, "Even in this field, missionaries were the pioneers in organizing medical relief and establishing hospitals and dispensaries for women and children in India. The first medical woman in India, Miss Clara Swain, came from America in 1869. . . . ."

Perhaps one of the most picturesque yet dynamic women to come into political prominence has been Begum Shah Nawaz of the Punjab, coming directly from the Mohammedan *purdah* group into the active political life of the nation. She was a very influential member of the Round Table Conference. Just before sailing for London to attend this conference she came out of *purdah*. Since that date she has been a progressive and hard-working member of the Punjab Legislative Assembly and a tireless worker in all reforms dealing with the advancement of women.

Every Christian woman is proud that in the early days of pioneering for reforms relating to women, there was Pundita Ramabai, who was a lone voice calling in the wilderness. That voice, like the coming of a single swallow, certainly did not mean that summer had come. Yet that voice was the first and we rejoice in the fact. Many of the present-day leaders in this work received inspiration from her.

Belonging to a later date was Susie Sorabji, a prominent Christian educationalist of western India. She always took her place with the utmost ease and charm in the great gatherings of Indian women. There is in the city of Poona a road named "The Susie Sorabji Road" in her memory. The influential institution, St. Helena's, where for so many years she labored, continues to be a center of genuine influence.

There are Christian women of outstanding ability throughout India today working side by side with other national leaders as college professors, teachers, doctors and legislators. Mrs. Mona Hensman, a woman of exceeding charm and personality, who has served as president of the National Young Women's Christian Association of India, is now working effectively as an able legislator in the upper house of the Madras Legislative Assembly.

Increasingly the men and women of India today are thinking in terms of constitutional government. This is not a natural product of India's rich and varied heritage, but it is the expected result from her association with Britain during the past century. In the Provincial Legislative Assemblies under the new constitution women are being welcomed as members. In the United Provinces Mrs. Ranjit S. Pandit, sister of the leading nationalist, Jawaharlal Nehru, has been chosen Minister of Public Health. She is a woman of charming personality and real ability. The fact that her children are in a Christian school, which the majority of the American missionary children of India attend, is indicative of her broad-minded attitude.

GREAT RELIGIOUS PROBLEMS

As you think with other minds in the succeeding chapters of more detailed facts and more concrete incidents concerning this miracle of changing India, you will become increasingly aware of the many perplexing questions which must be faced. India, sharing the upheaval of a troubled world which tends to reject all religions, is doubtless the most religious of all lands, and yet her religions have often been her greatest barrier to progress. Both nationalism and reform demand a change which may become catastrophic. What adjustments must the Christian church make to meet this situation?

Communism here finds fertile soil for growth. Will Government under the new Constitution be able so to coordinate its constructive factors as to maintain orderly development while conserving cherished principles and privileges for all communities?

Sixty million Untouchables are on the move from their semi-slavery of the centuries. Christian teaching and service have awakened in them new desires for religious, social, and material welfare. Should they turn to Christ, what preparation is required in the Christian church to meet adequately this unprecedented demand?

The divisions in the church are gradually being healed through close cooperation in service, facing staggering difficulties and opportunities. What is now most necessary and expedient to hasten a united church?

An increasing number of educated women are gradually awakening their slumbering sisters to share the light of a new day. What more can be done to insure that this freedom will be truly Christian and wholesome in every respect?

Because of certain patent reasons the Christian church has become too dependent on the West. What are the immediate next steps towards remedying these defects, developing its own self-reliance and a deepened passion for India's redemption?

Many have lost the keenness of a truly missionary passion. As one looks afresh at Christ, then at the far-reaching achievements, the needs and the open doors of opportunity in this land of India, can the loss of interest be worthily justified?

We missionaries labor in India today in one of the ripest harvest fields the world has ever afforded. The sacrificial investment of Christian personality and money are bearing fruit worthy of deepest gratitude. Changes in the situation are demanding adjustments in policy. These adjustments are often not easy, yet they are being made. But more than the need of adjustment in policy is the need of a fresh inflow of Christian light and life, producing transformed character. After years of study of comparative religion and with full appreciation of the achievements of science and art, it is clearer today than ever that Jesus Christ moves supreme in the stream of human living. Our supreme purpose in India is to introduce Him. We labor that men may wholeheartedly become his followers. But we also rejoice at every penetration of his life-giving rays into the reform movements and other religions. His dynamic is felt when he enters. His vitalizing power remains unmeasured. His transforming friendship is a sure solvent for otherwise impossible problems. He has awakened these new movements. Their destiny is safest in his hands.

We see in our dream India a united nation, with Christ supreme. The miracle of India for us does not merely mean a politically or geographically united India, but an India melted together by the transforming power of Jesus Christ.

"Dreamer of Dreams! We take the taunt with gladness,
    Knowing that God beyond the years you see,
Hath wrought the dreams that count with you for madness,
    Into the substance of the life to be."

CHAPTER II

THE UNTOUCHABLES

By J. WASKOM PICKETT

THE dramatic announcement from a small town in Western India in October, 1935, that ten thousand Untouchables had denounced the Hindu religion as responsible for their degradation and oppression, and had resolved to adopt the religion which, upon inquiry by their leaders, was found to possess the largest values for them, was recognized around the world as news of vast importance and arresting human interest. When this was followed by the announcement that the Untouchables throughout India were invited to join the revolt against Hinduism and the quest for a satisfying faith and that many thousands of them were doing so, world attention was focused upon these underprivileged sons and daughters of India as it had never been before. If by now casual readers have forgotten, the thoughtful remember and inquiry persists.

"Who are the Untouchables? Why and to whom are they 'untouchable'? Will missionaries touch them?" These and nine other questions about the people who are the subject of this chapter were put to the writer recently by a famous radio news commentator who immediately added, "No subject I have discussed in twelve months has excited more interest than the news from India about the Untouchables." This expert's statement about popular interest in the Untouchables has been amply confirmed.

WHY "UNTOUCHABLES"?

The word "untouchable" means exactly what it appears to mean. Those to whom the word is applied are not to be touched. Contact with the body or clothes of one of them causes pollution. Even accidental contact requires a ceremonial cleansing and a bath. Deliberate contact is often regarded as a cause for outcasting.

But in India the word is not in favor in all circles. Many other words are used to denote approximately the same groups, though one name may narrow and another widen the limits of those included. "Depressed classes" has been widely used. However, some may be accounted "depressed" who are not treated as Untouchables.

A few years ago strong objection began to be taken here and there within the ranks of these oppressed classes to the terms by which they were known. This led to the introduction of such names as Adi-Dravidas, or original Dravidians, and Adi-Hindus, or original Hindus. Many Untouchable castes moved to adopt new caste names. These efforts have stimulated the higher caste Hindus and even Governments to propose new names. Mr. Gandhi coined "Harijan," which he defines as "God's people." To this Dr. Ambedkar and many others object, declaring that "Harijan" means not "God's people" but "Krishna's people," and implies that they are bound to Hinduism. Provincial governments are trying "Scheduled Castes," which means "castes included in a schedule prepared by Government of those that require special protection and assistance," and "Exterior Castes," which means "castes not included in the framework of the Hindu village community."

Today many Untouchables are protesting against all names that hide or ignore the facts about their oppressions. "Don't try to fool us and quiet your conscience by calling us by less offensive names. Deal justly with us. That's more difficult, but nothing else will satisfy our demands," said one Untouchable recently. Another has spoken even more strongly: "Don't try to protect yourselves from the storm of our wrath and the world's contempt by coining new names to camouflage your cruelties. We won't accept verbal caresses from people to whom we remain in fact untouchable. You can't compensate or atone in words for the inhuman oppression which you still inflict upon us."

What It Means To Be an Untouchable

A young man of some education gave this statement of his own experience of untouchability: "We are made to live outside of the village. We cannot draw water from any well unless it be our own, and in our village we have none, but must wait beside the well until some one consents to draw water for us. The barbers won't cut our hair, the washermen won't wash our clothes, the merchants won't allow us to examine any goods in their shop. When we walk in the street people avoid us and shrink even from our shadows. We cannot enter the temples or the schools. The more religious our Hindu neighbors are the more afraid they seem to be of a touch from one of us. I have been beaten twice by order of the big men of my village for my impudence in ignoring my status as an Untouchable. My mother was kicked so severely that two ribs were broken and she had a miscarriage, because she inadvertently touched a young man when she tripped over an obstruction in the street. And instead of prosecuting the man who kicked her the police took ten rupees from my father on threat of charging that my mother had assaulted the young man."[1]

THE ORIGINS OF UNTOUCHABILITY

No one can describe with certainty the process by which untouchability developed. Many considerations have contributed to its origin and growth. Color and race are among them. The Untouchables are chiefly

---

[1] W. H. Wiser, "The Economics of Poverty," *The Indian Witness,* August 19, 1937, p. 518.

from among pre-Aryan aboriginal tribes and are darker than the Aryans. Color and race prejudice were strong in the ancient Aryan's mind and he determined to prevent associations that might lead to the marriage of his children or children's children with the darker race. Moreover the darker races had been subjugated in warfare and that fact contributed to their enslavement and the contempt of which untouchability was born. Through the centuries difference in social patterns, in cultural and economic levels, in moral standards, in occupations, in eating habits and in religious concepts and practices have influenced its development. The Aryan higher castes have been repelled by some of the practices of the Untouchables, notably their eating of the flesh of the sacred cow, and of animals that have died of old age or disease.

It must not be supposed that the Untouchables' social patterns were all inferior or their moral standards all lower than those of their oppressors, but only that they were different and were regarded as barbarous. The Untouchables allowed widow re-marriage, the higher castes did not. The higher castes adopted child-marriage, the Untouchables continued for centuries the custom of post-puberty marriage. Female infanticide was largely confined to the higher castes, and *sati,* the burning alive of widows on the funeral pyres of their husbands, was entirely confined to them. The Untouchables sometimes allowed a woman to divorce her husband, the higher castes never did. The double standard of personal morality characterized the upper classes only.

EFFECT OF OCCUPATIONAL RESTRICTIONS

Occupation has had more to do with the maintenance than with the origins of untouchability. Certain castes have been restricted to occupations that are held in contempt, such as work in leather, disposing of carcasses, and cleaning privies. With occupations made hereditary, and with eating, drinking and all kinds of friendly social relationships permitted only within the borders of one's own caste, a situation has developed which can hardly be imagined by people in other lands. Take for example the case of privy cleaners, commonly called Sweepers. Not only are they compelled to earn their living in this way but all their social relationships are with Sweepers. All their relatives do that work and every "respectable" occupation is closed to them. Moreover all their ancestors for a thousand years or more have been Sweepers, unless it be that somewhere in the line one has entered who became a Sweeper because he was excluded from a higher caste for some misdemeanor and chose this occupation rather than starve.

It is sometimes supposed that the Sweepers do not find their occupation trying, having been hardened thereto by generations of experience. Inquiry indicates that for many of them it is most difficult. A Sweeper woman recently reported that it took her six years to acquire sufficient control to do her work. That woman is now a Christian and an efficient, cultured school teacher; her daughter is in high school, apparently headed for college. Had the mother remained a Hindu, both she and her daughter would have been restricted to such joys in life as comport with the life of Sweepers.

NOT DISTINGUISHED BY DIRT, STUPIDITY OR VICE

The question, "Why do you treat these people as 'Untouchables'?" addressed to a member of one of the oppressor castes, usually brings the reply that they are dirty, or stupid, or vicious, or that they must suffer for their misdeeds in past lives. The last answer takes us into the realm of theological speculation and need not be considered now. It is true that among the Untouchables many are dirty, some are stupid, and a few vicious. But these are not distinguishing characteristics. The dirt, stupidity and vice of an Indian village are by no means concentrated in the quarters of the Untouchables, nor are the clean, intelligent and right-living men and women all found in the quarters of the touchable castes.

Fundamentally the Untouchables are very much the same sort of people as their fellow citizens in India and their contemporaries in other countries. The differences that are apparent concern social patterns, institutions and traditions, and are all on the surface of life; the resemblances concern emotions, capacity and character and go to the heart of life. In an environment that is extraordinarily hostile to the cultivation of the social virtues most Untouchables are honorable, law-abiding and friendly. Where everything and everybody tells them that they are dirty, stupid and vicious, most of them have managed to retain a measure of self-respect, certain standards of cleanliness, intelligence and honor, and a capacity, mental and spiritual, that surprises all who have the opportunity to witness their response to the stimulus of the Christian gospel.

In fact, the Untouchables are distinguished from their fellows by nothing else so much as by the cruelties inflicted upon them. They are sentenced to life oppression for the crime of being born of their mothers. The guilt is not theirs but belongs to the court of Hindu public opinion that sentences them, and the community that enforces the sentence. The court and the community have been led into their crime by trust in the Code of Manu, the lawgiver of Hinduism.

SOME CHARACTERISTICS OF UNTOUCHABLES

Centuries of oppression have bred in the Untouchables certain mass characteristics, as, for example, a fatalistic acquiescence in poverty and illiteracy. Exceptions there are and probably always have been, but the pattern of hopeless surrender to grinding poverty and ignorance was thoroughly established in the consciousness of Untouchable masses until the stirring events of recent years.

Another characteristic has been fear. While the power of their masters and neighbors over them was unlimited they lived in abject fear of offending them. Even now, when a large measure of protection is afforded the depressed classes by law and by public opinion—which is improving rapidly—few Untouchables are entirely free from fear of the higher castes. Within a month we have heard fresh reports of tyrannical mistreatment for the following offences: (1) Keeping an umbrella up during a rainstorm in the presence of a Brahman; (2) riding past a village head-man on a bicycle; (3) wearing a clean shirt; and (4) calling oneself a Christian. For these "crimes" the offenders were punished as follows: (1) The umbrella was broken and thrown away; (2) the rider was abused verbally, threatened with a beating, and compelled to walk, leading his cycle, until out of sight; (3) the shirt was torn and dirt thrown over the boy who had dared to wear it; and (4) the man was compelled to do *begar,* forced labor without pay, for his landlord for two weeks during the harvest season, when otherwise he might have earned one-third of his whole year's income.

But fear of man is exceeded by fear of evil spirits. The Untouchables with exceptions which, happily, are increasing, are animists and many of them live in terror of spirits which they imagine to lurk in the trees, in gulleys or ravines, in deserted houses, old wells and places where the dead have been burned or buried. A man whose entire family is pathetically undernourished and clothed in rags may spend a week's wages to exorcise the devil that is causing his tooth to ache. A village Christian, converted from the Untouchables in 1936, told the writer that he had lived in terror of evil spirits all his life until he learned from members of his caste who had become Christians that evil spirits never troubled them, and that Jesus had cast out the evil spirits of many who believed on him.

One of the most tragic characteristics bred in the Untouchables by Hinduism is distrust and antagonism between castes. The Brahmans, administrators of the Hindu social system, have been masters of the technique of "divide and rule." The victims of the caste system have been induced by a graduated scale of disabilities to fight among themselves for their positions. One caste has sought to ease its sufferings at the expense of another. When a Christian movement begins in one of these castes the greatest difficulty is encountered in persuading the converts that the gospel must be preached to members of the other Untouchable castes. The converts are influenced by their Hindu caste heritage to seek the advancement of their own people by showing that they are superior to and do not associate with members of other Untouchable castes.

Numbers and Location

No one can say with assurance how many Untouchables there are in India. To get a correct figure would

require a special census conducted by master psychol-
ogists. One caste may be untouchable in one area but
not in another. In the cities, especially the larger port
cities, many people who in their villages would be
strictly untouchable have become associates of their
higher caste Hindu neighbors. On the other hand, a few
very strict Hindus count all Christians, including Europeans and Americans, as Untouchables. When other
names are used the numbers to whom they are applied
are raised or lowered within very wide limits. The following estimate has been made by a leader of the Untouchables:

Unapproachables	500,000
Untouchables	35,600,000
Depressed Classes	50,000,000

Unapproachables are now found only in parts of
southern India. Elsewere all signs of that most vicious
extension of untouchability have disappeared. But Untouchables are found in every part of the domain of
Hinduism. Historically it appears to be true that the acceptance of Hinduism has led always to the recognition
of certain classes of the population as Untouchables. In
areas where the central concepts of Hinduism have never
been accepted, as in certain tracts peopled exclusively
by aboriginal tribes, there is no sign of untouchability,
and in areas where Hinduism has been supplanted by
Islam the practice has withered and died.

THE HINDU RELIGION AND UNTOUCHABILITY

This leads directly to the question, "Is Hinduism, as a religion, responsible for untouchability?" To this question Mr. Gandhi answers, "No!" and Dr. Ambedkar replies, "Yes!" Mr. Gandhi vigorously condemns and assails untouchability and urges the Untouchables to remain Hindus. Dr. Ambedkar vigorously condemns and assails Hinduism as responsible for untouchability and advises the Untouchables to cast the Hindu religion, root and branch, from their hearts and lives. The former speaks as an upper caste Hindu who deplores untouchability as a sin of his caste colleagues; the latter speaks as an Untouchable who holds that the oppression which he and his fellows suffer is the logical result of the religious concepts Hinduism has imparted to their oppressors. Mr. Gandhi says the sin is in the heart of the higher caste Hindus. Dr. Ambedkar says it is in the heart of Hinduism.

The responsibility of Hinduism may be sought in two directions: its effect first upon the oppressor castes and second upon the oppressed. Perhaps the most central concepts in Hinduism are *karma* and rebirth. The first teaches that every act inexorably determines its reward or its punishment, the second that the soul experiences a long chain of births and lives, in each of which joys and sorrows, advantages and disadvantages, are determined by what has gone before. The linking together of these central concepts leads logically to the conclusion that, if the Untouchables suffer, the responsibility belongs not to their oppressors but to themselves for misdeeds in earlier incarnations. So it relieves the oppressor of any sense of wrong-doing and even produces in his mind a vague sense of working with eternal, infinite power to do justice. A Brahman priest told the writer recently that Christian missionaries are putting the Untouchables back fifty thousand incarnations by imparting to them teaching that makes them dissatisfied with Hinduism and ambitious for better conditions in which to live. "They should accept their sufferings meekly and in time they would be born as high caste Hindus. Perhaps after many thousands of years they might even be Brahmans."

The direct effect of these doctrines upon the minds of the Untouchables is even more harmful to them. Nothing that Hinduism has done to the Untouchables has been so devastating as teaching them to despise themselves. When we realize how much our conduct is influenced by the mental picture we form of ourselves, we can understand at least dimly the damage done to the Untouchables by making them believe that they are what they are, poor, illiterate, oppressed and despised, because of their sins. For Brahman philosophers and members of other beneficiary castes the concept of *karma* is pleasant enough, adding to their enjoyment of the good things of life and sense of divine favor; but to the

Untouchables it is appalling, for it adds to their misery a sense of utter vileness and depravity. It is probable that the influence of *karma* on the mind and spirit of the Untouchables has done them more harm than all other oppressions inflicted on them. It has robbed them of initiative, hope and self-respect.

In a North India village we engaged in the following conversation with an Untouchable:

Q. Who are you?

A. I'm a Sweeper.

Q. Are you a Christian?

A. No. I was born a Sweeper. I must die a Sweeper.

Q. But why not be a Christian?

A. For my sins I was made a Sweeper. I must not object. Can I change my *karma* and be born a Christian?

Q. Why not ask God to forgive your sins? He will do so and you can be born again in this life.

A. No. There is no forgiveness. I was very wicked or I would not have been born a Sweeper.

Q. Won't you send your children to the mission school? They can live better lives if they learn.

A. No! They, too, must suffer for their sins. They were born as Sweepers. If they try to be gentlemen it will only add to their sins.

REVOLTS

The victims of any social order are naturally more hospitable to ideas of change in that order than are those who profit by it. And when a social order that imposes hardships upon a section of the population rests upon religious concepts, as does the order associated with Hinduism, those concepts are less likely to hold the allegiance of the victims of that order than of its beneficiaries. So the centuries have brought many revolts against caste and *karma* and other perversions of truth that underlie both the social system and religious practice of Hinduism. While their leaders have sometimes come from high or middle castes, the rebels have been recruited in the main from the Untouchables. These revolts have even extended to military action. Moslem conquerors were often aided by Untouchables. The Battle of Plassey in 1757, which decided the issue of British rule in India, was won by Clive through the aid of an army of Dusadhs, and the Marathas were defeated in western India through the help of regiments of Mahars. Moslem predominance in the Punjab and in eastern Bengal has been achieved through mass movements of Untouchables to Islam, entire castes and tribes in some areas having joined the followers of the prophet of Arabia. Many Untouchables have also tried Sikhism, an eclectic religion compounded of Hindu and Islamic elements. This religion, which arose at the same time as the Protestant Reformation in Europe, denounces caste and idolatry and proclaims human brotherhood and the unity of God. In every province of India Christian converts have come mainly from the unprivileged classes,

Untouchables and aboriginal tribesmen. This is true despite the fact that missionary effort has been addressed mainly to the more privileged classes.

MISSIONARY POLICY

When missionaries arrived in India at the beginning of the modern era of Christian expansion they quite naturally gave primary attention to the Brahmans and those who shared with them in the control of society. The Brahmans were cultured, ready in speech and action, interested in philosophy and religion, and they controlled public life. The Untouchables, on the other hand, were untutored and uncouth, retiring, without a voice in public affairs, despised by their neighbors, inarticulate on the subject of religion, and reputed to be dirty and stupid. Small wonder that many missionaries concentrated entirely upon Brahmans, expecting through their conversion to win all classes to Christ. But few Brahmans responded as the missionaries hoped they would. Many were attracted by the character of Christ and professed admiration for his teaching, but saw in the gospel a menace to the exalted position of their caste. They preferred Hinduism with special privilege to Christianity with equality. Gradually, however, the Christian message reached the oppressed Untouchables and here and there, where hope was not dead, it was heard with gladness.

The largest movements have occurred among Telugu-speaking people. At the time of the Indian famine of 1876 Dr. John E. Clough, a Baptist missionary who had been trained as an engineer, took over a government contract for building a canal in South India, employing Untouchables for the work. "These unfortunate people were all deeply impressed with the fact that religious leaders should so unselfishly give help to all—regardless of caste, and asked to become Christians by thousands. On the third of July, 1878, six native pastors baptized two thousand two hundred and twenty-two people, and by the end of the year the number had grown to nine thousand six hundred and six, making the Ongole Baptist church the largest in the world. Within ten years, twenty-five thousand converts were baptized, and a remarkable transformation had taken place among the humble outcastes."[1]

GROUP RESPONSE

One feature of the response of the Untouchables to the preaching of the gospel puzzled the missionaries and caused some of them distress. That was group action. The missionaries in the main held to a very individualistic interpretation of conversion. They sought to bring individuals to personal faith, repentance and pardon through independent action. But the Untouchables frequently came in groups to ask for Christian instruction

---

[1] Anna C. Swain, *Youth Unafraid*, p. 96-101. New York, Baptist Board of Education, 1935.

or to profess Christian faith and seek divine pardon. The missionaries did not understand that people who were accustomed to group action in all affairs of common interest, having been trained from infancy to subordinate personal choice to group decision, could not be expected to act otherwise in responding to the gospel. Urge a man with that background of group control to act independently in a matter as vital as changing religious allegiance and you outrage his senses of propriety and ethics. Insist that he abandon his fellows to become a Christian without first consulting them and trying to persuade them to act with him, and if he consents, he will start his Christian life with the handicap of a sense of guilt. Group decision is for most of India's Untouchables and for many others the most natural way of approach to Christ and, despite dangers, is much to be preferred to independent action. The preservation of social integration is desirable in the interests of the convert's own spiritual life and of his influence upon his associates.

THE POWER OF PREACHING

The preaching of the cross of Christ has proved to be the power of God for multitudes of the Untouchables. It is the perfect antidote to the poison which Hindu teaching about *karma*, caste and reincarnation has injected into their souls. The assurances that Christ offers salvation to them on exactly the same terms as to the Brahman or the American, that God is not against them for their sins but is for them against their sins, and that, instead of being a despised, worthless people, they become, by virtue of their acceptance of Christ as Lord and Savior, the pioneers of a new social order, work radical changes in their outlook on life. These assurances are not made real and effective to them by the mere telling. Such words may fall upon the ear and be conveyed to the mind without being heard in the final sense of which Jesus spoke when at the end of a sermon he said, "If any man have ears to hear, let him hear." But preaching that arrests attention and leads to believing worship has this effect.

TRANSFORMATION OF UNTOUCHABLES

Communities of Untouchables where the Christian gospel has been received and worship established on lines that are meaningful and vital to the congregation of believers reveal a transformation that is remarkable and convincing. We have seen entire villages in which the despised Untouchables have been so enriched in personality and so thoroughly reconstructed in character and conduct that erstwhile oppressors have accepted them as counselors in religion. A Brahman who recently applied for baptism and entrance to the church made this statement to the writer: "The Untouchables of this village were utterly vicious and degraded; they were illiterate, stupid, filthy and vile. In twenty years they have become honorable, clean, intelligent and God-fearing. What no Hindu thought possible has been performed before our eyes. I know Christ is real. I love him for what he has done to the Untouchables. I want him to work a like change in my heart. My caste will oppress me but I will find peace and salvation."

ASSETS OF THE NATION

Scattered over India today are tens of thousands of Christians, men and women, engaged in public service as teachers, officials, doctors, nurses and preachers, whose parents or grandparents endured the oppressions and exhibited the characteristics common to the Untouchables. They who but for the coming of Christ in their homes would have been liabilities to the nation, poverty-stricken, despised, illiterate, diseased and dirty, a menace to every national interest, are among the nation's most valuable assets.

Picture a gathering of citizens in an Indian city, called together to plan a fight against tuberculosis. The chairman is a Moslem; the chief speaker a Hindu official of the Board of Health. On the platform with these men sits the principal of the Christian or mission high school in which both the chairman and the speaker were students two decades ago. Both men pay public tribute to the principal, their former teacher, as the man whose example and instruction had aroused in them the purpose to serve their fellow men. And who was that school principal? He was born in a Sweeper's hovel beside an open sewer. His father had lived and died as an illiterate, superstitious, undernourished, often sick and ever despised Untouchable. From that environment and that fate Christ lifted the son and made him the respected teacher, the beloved inspirer of youth, the friend of the sick and the suffering, a pioneer of the kingdom of brotherhood in the land of caste.

No service of Christ to India through the modern missionary movement has more truly enriched the nation than the changed status he has brought to Untouchable women who have become his disciples. In one large city one hundred and thirty Christian women of a single church, practically all products of a recent mass movement of Untouchables, are teaching in municipal schools. A Hindu school inspector said to the writer, "Education for girls in this generation would be impossible but for Christian women teachers." In one South India town a Bible woman from an Untouchable caste has organized a church consisting of more than thirty women who have been converted through her work. In a rural community a servant woman has been given a permanent seat in the pulpit of a church containing converts from twelve castes. Through her efforts the revival occurred in which this church was born. They count her a saint.

THE GROWTH OF CHRISTIAN MASS MOVEMENTS

The principle of group action in religion, as we have already indicated, was encountered in the earliest years of Protestant missions in India. But the policies generally adopted by missionaries placed many restrictions upon the spread of Christian faith by that principle. Fear that converts would be led astray by their associates led many missionaries to protect them by isolation upon the mission compound and by a paternalism that resulted in the adoption of Western social patterns and modes of life. However, in the latter part of the eighteenth century, a wider movement took place in the far south which could not be dealt with so thoroughly. So many groups confessed faith in Christ that they had to be allowed to remain in their homes, and thereby escaped much of the denationalizing effect of the erroneous policy of the well intentioned missionary pioneers. The results were so good that the wiser ones among the missionaries revised their policies. Since then like movements have taken place in most of the provinces and in many cases have been whole-heartedly encouraged as their superior results have been recognized. The Census of 1931 shows that the Indian Christian population increased in the preceding decade by 1,542,684 persons. A study of the areas of large growth has convinced the writer that this increase represents an annual average accession to the Christian community during that decade, through group movements by the underprivileged, of at least 125,000. Since 1931 the rate of growth of these movements has been accelerated, despite intense nationally organized and directed opposition. There must now be many millions among the Untouchables who know something of these Christward movements and are considering whether they and their local groups should follow the trail of those who have abandoned the old ways of shame and moved toward Christ.

MR. GANDHI AND CHRISTIAN CONVERSION

That opposition to the conversion of the Untouchables should be voiced by Mr. Gandhi puzzles many Christian people. They have admired him and thought of him as an unbaptized Christian, or very nearly that. However puzzling or incredible it may seem, it is true that Mr. Gandhi is aggressively opposing all Christian work for the Untouchables that seeks to influence them in favor of conversion. His paper, *The Harijan,* contains frequent articles from his pen criticizing Christians who undertake to influence Untouchables in favor of Christianity. With less than his customary sagacity Mr. Gandhi recently declared that the Untouchables are no more able to decide what religion is best for them than a cow would be. When this statement was criticized Mr. Gandhi sought to appease the Untouchables by widening it to take in many higher caste Hindus, including Mrs. Gandhi. He considers that missionaries who are unable to persuade him and his associates to become Christians should not approach the illiterate and unsophisticated Untouchables. One of the distinguished leaders of the Untouchables on reading Mr. Gandhi's remark described

TYPICAL OUTCASTE SECTION OF AN INDIAN VILLAGE

H. R. Ferger

A SUNDAY SCHOOL FOR NON-CHRISTIAN CHILDREN IN
TANNERS VILLAGE, NIPANI

it as "the crowning insult" and added, "The higher castes who have oppressed us for centuries now find in Mr. Gandhi a spokesman who forbids the messengers of the Savior to communicate with us." Another such leader calls Mr. Gandhi "the public enemy number one of my people," and claims that Mr. Gandhi's program of opening the temples of Hinduism for the Untouchables would complete their enslavement to the exploiting classes. "In only one area of our lives have we been free. We were not allowed to enter the temples of Hinduism and so hitherto could worship as we pleased."

In fairness to Mr. Gandhi it should be remembered that while opposing conversion he is vigorously fighting against Untouchability and has inspired a great army of his fellow religionists to help meet the social and economic needs of the Untouchables. He welcomes co-operation of Christians in seeking to ameliorate the condition of the oppressed so long as they do not seek to induce a change of faith or, perhaps we might say fairly, so long as they do not encourage the renunciation of the Hindu name.

"Nor should we overlook the peculiar relation developed in India between the religion to which one is accredited and his social pattern, the civil law by which he is governed and his political relationships. In several provinces Christians vote in a communal electorate and every conversion to Christianity reduces the numerical strength of the general electorate in which Hindus preponderate."

THE EMERGENCE OF DR. AMBEDKAR

The most able and dynamic leader of the Untouchables is Dr. Bhim Rao Ambedkar, principal of the Government Law College in Bombay and leader of the United Labor Party in the Bombay Legislative Assembly. Dr. Ambedkar's career is stranger and more romantic than any tale of fiction. Although his father, as a soldier in the Indian army, lived on a plane definitely above the common level of Untouchables, when the son presented himself for enrollment in a government primary school the Hindu teacher tried to persuade him to go home. An appeal to a government official resulted in his enrollment, but the surly teacher made him sit apart from the other children and refused to instruct him. Nevertheless, encouraged only by his father, he was determined to learn and year by year, fighting for his opportunity, he advanced from class to class while the higher caste boys, whom the teacher and the public encouraged, and who persisted in treating him as untouchable and stupid, dropped out. A majority of them never learned to read but went back into their villages to boast of their superiority and to take up from their elders the age-old oppression of the "inferior" castes.

High school and college the determined young man took in his stride. No subject held him back or presented any terrors for him. The teacher who first objected to enrolling him had stalled at the seventh class. Other teachers who had insulted him, watched in bewilderment as he swept easily past them. When he was graduated from college, seemingly at the end of his formal study, the impossible happened. A Hindu prince, the Gaekwar of Baroda, offered him a scholarship for foreign study. He proceeded to Edinburgh, thence to London, later to Columbia University in New York, Bonn in Germany and back to London. At length he returned to India a master of arts, a doctor of philosophy, a doctor of science and a barrister.

DISILLUSIONMENT

While abroad he had, as most students from India do, idealized his homeland. The oppressions of his youth receded to the hinterland of his memory and he dreamed of returning to India to be proudly acclaimed for the record he had made and the honors he had won. A cruel disillusionment awaited him. To the caste Hindus he remained an Untouchable. He was unable to rent quarters, either for office or residence. His benefactor, the Gaekwar, offered him honorable employment but the subjects of His Highness were less liberal. He resigned and went to Bombay.

This move brought upon him a severe temptation. Bombay, as the chief port of entrance for Western influence and a commercial metropolis, is more inclined than the rest of the country to accept a man for what he is, without inquiring about his caste or background. He thought of opening an office as a lawyer, isolating himself from his people, and building up a practice by sheer ability, with his clients ignorant of his Untouchable origin. While in the West he had become an agnostic and a confirmed secularist. He had resolved to leave religion alone and as far as possible dismiss it from consideration. But he possessed ideals and they could not easily be dismissed. The thought of abandoning his people disturbed him. "Why," he asked, "have I been so fortunate? Why have I alone of India's Untouchables received such opportunities? Surely not for my personal advantage only! I have a duty to perform. I must help those who suffer the persecution from which I in a large measure have escaped."

So he went to Bombay as an Untouchable and with the practice of law began simultaneously social service for his people. This led him quickly into politics and six years after his return to India he was appointed to represent the Untouchables at the Round Table Conference in London where he joined representatives of the British Parliament in planning a new constitution for the Government of India. Here he came into dramatic conflict with Mr. Gandhi. The latter, sitting in the Conference as the sole representative of the Indian National Congress, challenged Dr. Ambedkar's right to speak in behalf of the Untouchables and claimed that right as his own. Many in England and India were amazed at the spectacle of the young Untouchable, only six years out of college, and probably the youngest member of the Conference, opposing Mr. Gandhi as no other member of the Conference dared to do. But while others wondered the Untouchables thrilled. They left no doubt of their choice between the antagonists. In hundreds of massed meetings they declared Ambedkar to be their leader and spokesman.

THE FIGHT FOR A SHARE IN LAW-MAKING

The issue on which Dr. Ambedkar and Mr. Gandhi fought was whether the Untouchables and other depressed classes should acquire the right to elect their own representatives in the legislatures, or should be included in a general electorate. Mr. Gandhi argued that separate representation is unnecessary and inconsistent with democratic principles. Dr. Ambedkar argued that it is essential to the welfare of the oppressed, that without it democracy would mean delivering them into the hands of their enemies. When the Conference could not agree on the issue of communal representation the Prime Minister was made arbiter and awarded a separate franchise and a specified number of reserved seats to the Untouchables, the Moslems and certain other minor communities. Dr. Ambedkar had won against Mr. Gandhi! A few months later when both were back in India they clashed again with the same result. Dr. Ambedkar was now established as a powerful force in the political life of the nation.

AN EXPERIENCE WITH PRAYER

During the Round Table Conference Dr. Ambedkar had an experience which registered and strengthened a changing attitude toward religion. When the pressure was upon him to yield to Mr. Gandhi he prayed. He did not want to pray. He thought that he did not believe in prayer and was rather ashamed to pray. But he could not help praying. And as he prayed something happened. He was conscious of a release of power and a clarification of mind. He felt that the future of tens of millions of his people depended upon his action and that the course he had purposed to take was right. For him the issue was no longer in doubt. He felt that a wisdom greater than his own and a power outside of him and greater than his had come to his help.

RELIGION CONDEMNED AND RELIGION REQUIRED

Returning to India his thought turned instinctively and persistently to religion. He found the religious concepts of his people interfering with all of his efforts to open up new avenues of opportunity for them. His hopes of accomplishment through social service and political activity shrank as they were subjected to trial. The conviction formed that the fundamental need of his people was a new body of religious concepts, a new set of ideas about themselves in relation to society and to God. He resolved to study the great religions and to call upon his people throughout India to renounce Hinduism as the agent of their oppression. He carefully prepared the way and at a political conference of Untouchables in October, 1935, he denounced Hinduism in words that electrified India and are apparently destined to live down the centuries. But more significant, he went on to declare his purpose to adopt some other religion. "It is not my fault that I was born a Hindu. But to die as a Hindu would be a disgrace. I will adopt a religion which is no enemy to my self-respect." His audience of more than ten thousand enthusiastically responded. They rose and cheered and whooped with delight that such a leader had appeared among them. Then they solemnly renounced Hinduism and pledged that they would follow their leader into whatever religion he would choose as best for them.

Souls for Auction?

As this news spread great excitement developed in India. Hundreds of gatherings of Untouchables were held, in many of which resolutions supporting Dr. Ambedkar were adopted. Hindu politicians were alarmed, fearing a mass exodus from Hinduism. Moslems were elated, visualizing many millions added to their numbers. Many Christians were bewildered, puzzled by the declaration and fearing that religion would be dragged down to the level of competitive bidding for purely nominal adherents.

Some of Dr. Ambedkar's early declarations were unfortunately worded. They suggested to many readers that he was either engaged in a political maneuver or was expecting to recommend acceptance of the faith whose representatives promised the most in material inducements. Without his approval certain minor leaders, professing agreement with his purpose, organized conferences in which speakers presented claims for their faiths. Abroad there was talk of sixty million people simultaneously adopting a new religion.

Dr. Ambedkar is being subjected to terrific pressure to desist from his efforts. Hindu leaders assure him that he has already accomplished what they assume to be his real purpose, namely to compel a reform within Hinduism. He has announced no decision. In the meantime many of his followers are growing restless and asking him to indicate at least the direction of his thinking.

The Great Decision

What will Dr. Ambedkar decide? How will his decision be received? We cannot anticipate his announcement. He will make it in his own time and in his own way. It is known, however, that he is eagerly studying Christianity. He has spoken of the appeal which the Gospels and certain passages in the Epistles of St. Paul made to his heart. He has also criticized the Christian church as he has met it in western India. Will he advise his people to turn to Christ, or to Islam, Buddhism or

Sikhism, or will he go no further with his plans? These questions we cannot answer.

THE CHRISTIAN PROSPECT

But whatever Dr. Ambedkar may do, the Christian church has a duty to perform and an opportunity to utilize in connection with the Untouchables. Neither began with Dr. Ambedkar's declaration. The Untouchables have always needed Christ and whenever the gospel has been widely proclaimed among them some have accepted him. They are turning to him now in larger numbers than ever before. There are many indications that increasing numbers will seek to know him in the years that are just ahead. Hardly a week passes without news reaching the writer of new groups asking for Christian instruction and leadership in worship. As we have been writing this chapter an appeal has come for three evangelists to be placed in an area twenty miles from the nearest mission station, where eight hundred people of Dr. Ambedkar's own caste have declared their desire to follow Christ and to bring relatives and friends to him. During the same time an appeal has come from an Indian minister for advice on how to deal with thirty families who have begun to call themselves Christians though they are not baptized, have had no instruction, and live so far away that no regular ministerial service can be provided for them.

Radical changes in the attitude of Hindus toward the

Untouchables are undoubtedly taking place. The results may be more apparent in discussions in the legislatures and the press than in the experience of the average victim of untouchability. But no competent student of social trends in India can doubt that Hinduism is going to make a serious effort to appease the anger of the Untouchables. Mr. Gandhi's Harijan Sevak Sangh (Society for the Service of the Untouchables) is already making an organized effort to that end. An Untouchable leader who has been in close touch with Moslem propagandists said to the writer a few weeks ago, "The Moslems give me an impression that they want us for political purposes of their own and that they are ready to do much for us. Everywhere they will fight to end our oppressions. They will compel the Hindus to stop this foolishness of forbidding us to draw water from the village wells. Nevertheless, taking the long view, we see that it would be good neither for us nor for the country, for us to become Moslems."

The Christian church in India is more missionary minded today than it has ever been. And its missionary efforts are directed toward the Untouchables more generally than ever before. But the Christian task in India belongs to all Christian people who are able to help, and the Untouchables need the love, the prayers and the cooperation of representatives of all who love the Lord Jesus in the churches of North America and Europe.

CHAPTER III

INDIA'S RURAL MILLIONS

By ALICE B. VAN DOREN

"As go the villages, so goes India."—KENYON A. BUTTERFIELD

A HIGH-POWERED motor car attempts to pass through the narrow streets of a large Indian village, but the power is of no effect and the engine stalls, for it finds itself in the midst of a traffic jam. Just ahead, and traveling in the opposite direction, are two high carts with heavy wooden wheels; one cart moves to the right and the other to the left so that the entire road is blocked. From behind comes a herd of gigantic black buffaloes, successfully blocking the borders of the highway. A mixed flock—or herd—of sheep and goats, several stray hens, and here and there a bright-eyed toddling child fill in the cracks and crevices of the traffic. A droning sound is heard over-head and immediately a crowd of men and boys collect from no-where in particular to gaze upward at a small speck which presently develops into an Imperial Airways plane carrying the mail to Calcutta.

So this is India; the air mail at two hundred miles an hour; the motor at sixty; the ox-cart at two, all functioning at the same point of time and space. What else can this be but an era of confusion?

While the motor waits for the traffic jam to break up, we search for other signs of the confusion of eras. Yonder is a tailor's shop; the man's bare feet are working the treadle of a Singer sewing machine. From the house of the village headman comes the sound of a cheap and tinny phonograph—first an ancient and beloved Indian tune sung by a new musical "star"; then some recent jazz from a London music hall. In the general shop of the bazaar, next to the bamboo baskets of grains and condiments, are all sorts of products from the industrialized countries of the West—galvanized iron buckets supplanting brass pots, hurricane lanterns from Germany, matches from Sweden, cloth from Manchester, cheap toys from Japan, Standard Oil from New York.

Just at this moment new sounds attack the ear—a laboring engine, the grinding of brakes, an incessant and deafening horn. A motor bus carrying twice the legitimate number of passengers, and with its top loaded with vast accretions of tin trunks, bundles, buckets, cooking pots, and household goods of infinite variety, whirls precariously around a corner and by some miracle of Providence arrives in the midst of babies, buffaloes, and hens without destroying a single life. In the wheezing, overcrowded bus we see the climax of rural change in India. An occasional airplane may fly overhead and cause wonder to the bazaar; a high-powered car or a humble Ford may pass through the streets and divert the inhabitants as they watch the strange dress and ways of its occupants; but the bus is the villager's own possession. In it he travels—at twenty miles an hour instead of two. In it the peasant goes to the town and the town with its new ways and alluring products comes to the countryside.

DRASTIC CHANGES IN VILLAGE LIFE

From this impact of the machine age upon a primitive rural tradition, confusion results. New desires impinge upon ancient poverty. People desire to travel upon busses and trains, to possess toy balloons, electric torches, phonographs, and bicycles, to attend the motion pictures in the nearest town. The new urge is there, but not the means of fulfillment, for there has been no increase in the eight cents or the handful of grain that constitutes the daily income. If the new desires are to be fulfilled, either the peasant must sink deeper into the slough of debt, or he must emigrate to the city and be absorbed into the ranks of the mill workers, or too often into the proletarian army of the unemployed. Or if he comes from the emigrant sections of India—the Tamil and Telugu countries of the south, Gujarat on the west, or Chota Nagpur on the east—he will trek further afield, to the tea gardens of Assam or Ceylon, the rubber plantations of the Malay Peninsula, or the mines and cities of South Africa. A survey of a very small Christian village in South India revealed the fact that members of its homes had wandered all the way to Burma on the east and the Persian Gulf on the west.

But changes in the village are not merely physical, they are psychological as well. A keen student of village life writes as follows: "The other day I saw two sewing machines in a Chamar (leather-worker's) house in a village, and I found a Chamar woman sewing for some patrons. This transfer of the seamster's duties to a leather-worker is a matter of more significance to the existing social and economic order than if I had found good cattle, good food, a well ventilated house, a fodder cutter, and many other things which our rural reconstructionists are introducing in village homes. In another village I found leather-workers selling *ghi* (clarified butter) in the village. This has been the prerogative of the milkmen caste and no leather-worker would dare to leave his leather work or field work for such a business. . . . . Upsetting the existing social and economic order is a matter with endless implications."[1]

What is bringing about these changes in thought and action? Causes are many and complex, and to go into them deeply is beyond the scope of this chapter or its author. Yet some are clearly evident. First there are those very material changes described above—the impact of western science and trade upon the life of the Indian peasant.

LEADERS OF CHANGING CONDITIONS

There are also the rapid political and social changes which are churning to the bottom the thought and life of

---

[1] W. H. Wiser, "Economics of Poverty."

the Indian nation. First in order of time comes Mr. Gandhi with his fight against untouchability—the system that segregates the outcaste from the amenities and social privileges of the Indian community somewhat as the social system of the Southern States segregates the Negro from the life of his white neighbors. Mr. Gandhi is himself living in a village and experimenting with subsidiary industries such as spinning, weaving, bee-keeping, etc., for the benefit of outcaste as well as caste folk.

Dr. Ambedkar, quite unsatisfied with either the scope or speed of Mr. Gandhi's reforms, has led the revolt of his fellow castemen, demanding complete withdrawal from the Hindu system. I have myself attended a mass meeting of a thousand or more outcastes, in which Dr. Ambedkar's picture, carried in a palanquin, was given the place of honor on the platform while shouts and cheers announced victory for his campaign and "boycott" for the caste system.

Thirdly, Pundit Nehru comes forward with a program of action that is socialistic as well as political. His ideal is to free the Indian peasant from capitalistic domination, Indian as well as European. He knows village life both from theoretical study and from actual experience, is organizer and leader of peasants' associations, and is regarded with passionate devotion by the North India peasantry who throng the courtyards of his town house in Allahabad. His magnetic personality and strong influence in Congress circles are putting the

claims of the villager before the country with a new
forcefulness. He declares that mere political independence would only shift economic domination from the
British to the Indian capitalist and would achieve little
unless accompanied by a reform of the whole economic
system.

At the same time, Government is awakening to its responsibilities for the uplift of rural India. Mr. F. L.
Brayne, a government official of the Punjab, has spent
many years in carrying out a practical program of rural
reconstruction. Though this program has suffered from
too great a measure of external authority and compulsion, and is apt to come to a halt when the external
pressure is removed, yet much has been done in the demonstration of hygienic and agricultural improvement.
The present Viceroy, Lord Linlithgow, has a genuine
interest in the welfare of rural India, particularly in the
improvement of village cattle. He has "set the fashion"
for presenting stud bulls of good breed to groups of
villages to improve the quality of the local cattle.

Apart from Nationalists and government officials,
there are other instigators of change who have worked
in less conspicuous ways during the past century. Christian missionaries and Christian Indians have found their
teaching accepted by hundreds of thousands of village
folk, a majority of them outcastes at the very bottom of
the social scale. The message of God's equal love and
care for all his children and of the brotherhood taught

MODERN METHODS OF PLOUGHING. AGRICULTURAL INSTITUTE, ALLAHABAD, INDIA

John L. Goheen

SANGLI MOVABLE SCHOOL—ALL LOADED

by Christ has put into the life of the Untouchable a
leaven whose working knows no limit. Though less conspicuous and sensational than these later manifestations,
the era of change started by Christian missions is now
causing the greatest social upheaval known in India's
history. The leaven is working, but it has not yet pene-
trated very far into the lump. Even the superficial changes
described in the opening paragraphs of this chapter
would not be found to any great extent in isolated villages back from the main roads that permit motor travel.

NEEDS OF VILLAGE LIFE: LITERACY

As we go on to consider the chief needs of the village,
a word of caution is not superflous. Village life does
not represent the whole of India. The Indian who loves
his country objects rightly to a description that deals only
with her submerged masses. In reading of rural needs let
us not forget India's heritage of art and culture and music,
her present-day scholarship, and the self-sacrificing efforts of her patriotic sons and daughters to solve this vast
problem of rural distress. However, the need is there, and
its removal calls for the help of all agencies—Nationalist,
Government and Christian.

Among the many needs of the villager literacy may be
placed foremost. Without the use of the "tools of learning" he is left helpless in his conflict with destructive
forces. Culture may be transmitted through oral tradition, through drama, and the song and tale of the bard;

but oral tradition cannot help the borrower to check up the money lender's falsified account, nor enable him to read the legal document that concerns his ownership of land. Oral tradition cannot keep him in touch with the movements of the modern world nor can it help to free him from the bonds of superstitious fear. Yet with all the talk that abounds concerning the promotion of literacy, according to the last census its advance in ten years has kept ahead of the population increase by only eight-tenths of one per cent. Dr. Frank C. Laubach estimates that at the present rate of increase it will require eleven hundred and fifty years for India to become as literate as Japan.

Many children who achieve a small degree of literacy in school, lose in a few years the little they have learned. It is generally supposed that in order to insure permanent literacy, a child must advance to the fourth class. Also the retention of literacy depends upon other factors —life among other literates, preferably in a literate home and the accessibility of easy and interesting reading material. In the case of the majority of village children, neither of these desirable conditions exists.

Another hindrance to literacy is the extreme complexity of the Indian alphabets—marvels of phonetic perfection but many of them with three hundred to five hundred characters, including vowels, consonants, and combinations which present a great obstacle to the would-be learner. Still another difficulty lies in the difference between the classical literary language of the school books, and the ordinary colloquial speech of the villager. If American first and second readers were written in the vocabulary and style of Shakespeare and Milton, American children might sympathize to a small degree with the difficulties of the child in the Indian village. Christian missions are feeling as never before their obligation to contribute to the spread of literacy, yet the percentage of literacy among Christians fell slightly within the past ten years, because of the mass influx of illiterate outcastes. Without Bible-reading Christians it is impossible to envisage a pure and spiritually minded church.

VILLAGE SCHOOLS

Ever since the visit to India of the Village Education Commission in 1920, there has been an effort among Indians and missionaries of vision to promote a new type of village school that will teach not only the tools of learning found in the Three R's; but will carry on such an activity program as will integrate the school with the life of the village and the home. The Christian school at Moga in the Punjab has been the pioneer institution in training village teachers for this type of education. So successful has it been that the Government Department of Education in the Punjab now sends its inspecting officers and headmasters to annual refresher courses at Moga, and the whole of primary education

in that great and progressive province has been led into
new ways through the efforts of this one school.

A personal letter from Western India tells of the following developments: "Our little town goes rural-
minded! Always has been so, but now more than ever.
The first sight to meet my eye as we drove through the
gates after an absence of seven months was the little
herd of graded Janmapari goats belonging to the girls'
school, grazing peacefully in the field. As we whizzed
by, I saw hens, clear white hens with fine red combs,
hens here, there, everywhere—the flocks of the school
by means of which the girls are being taught the possibilities in poultry. Then fields, all green with growing
grain; here the black buffalo, giving six *seers* (approximately quarts) of milk a day; there the white bullocks,
our draft animals; then more white hens and cocks—
this time the flock of the district missionary who sells
the graded stock, practically full-blooded leghorns,
into the villages as fast as calls come. Today he had
a call for 300 eggs and ten cocks! Then the girls'
school, more girls than ever, busier than ever, all
seemingly intent on some business in hand though
they find time to get into mischief. The chicken-rais-
ing, goat-keeping, sewing and cooking classes go on
even though the girls still have the regular government
curriculum. Then the library! For years it has been a
dream and yesterday one hundred and twenty-five persons made use of it. On its tables are magazines and

books in three languages. The room is light and airy; a pressure kerosene lamp makes it possible to keep it open in the evening. Now the request for courses in Rural Improvement has come from the people themselves through the library, next we hope to meet that need."

Among high schools, the one that has pioneered most fruitfully is Ushagram at Asansol, Bengal. Its lines of special activity include interests as diverse as Indian art on the one hand, and the installation of cheap septic tanks on the other. There are great numbers of other schools, that are working quietly in all parts of India to revolutionize the type of education for the village child. In general it may be said that elementary education has been more successful than secondary in achieving this change of emphasis. Elementary schools are less examination-centered, and less bound by the red tape of a Government-ordered curriculum. They are also closer to village life and conditions.

ADULT EDUCATION

But we in India are realizing with ever increasing clearness that education of children can never be enough. At first thought one feels that it ought to be enough, for children are the hope of the world. Why bother with adults whose habits and attitudes are already set; they will not live very long and "while there is death there is hope"—at least for the new generation.

But further consideration shows the fallacy in this superficial thinking. A child may be educated in a social
vacuum—many schools are best described by that word;
but he cannot live in a vacuum. That is the reason why
so many pupils who leave mission schools revert not
only into illiteracy but into primitive standards of life
and morals. A child cannot rise very far above his parents, a wife above her husband, or a husband above his
wife. In India even more than in the individualistic
West, the individual, the family and the social group
must move together. Adult education must accompany
child education; adult literacy, child literacy, if either is
to be permanent.

Dr. Frank Laubach of the Philippines, beginning his
work among the Moros of Mindanao, has developed a
method of teaching adults through which whole peoples
can readily become literate in their own language. He
recently spent several months in India and gave great
inspiration and help in carrying forward a nation-wide
campaign for the removal of illiteracy. Everywhere he
found keen interest, and an astonishing number of
people beginning to experiment, including both Christians and non-Christians. Says Dr. Laubach, "The new
approach works like magic. We have lessons in Marathi,
Hindi, Urdu, Tamil, Telugu, Bengali, Punjabi, Mal-
ialam and Kanarese. Each of these has its own distinct
alphabet. The Congress committee which works with
Mr. Gandhi asked me to sit with them in Allahabad to

discuss the new alphabet. The chairman and I worked out an alphabet that has only sixteen distinct sounds, and yet contains every letter they need. The new method which we have developed meets with the four requirements: rapid progress in learning; easy to teach without training; fascinating; cheap—two cents a book."[1] From conferences with interested groups there emerged certain definite needs and plans for the advance of literacy, among which are the following:

1. The need for simple and interesting methods for the rapid teaching of adults. Under Dr. Laubach's guidance, such methods have been discovered and applied to the production of inexpensive charts and primers, which have been printed and are now being experimented with.

2. The need for very simple reading material in an inexpensive form. This must be written in words familiar to the villager, and must deal with matters in which adults are naturally interested; readers for little children are not suitable. For the use of Christians and for evangelistic effort among non-Christians three gospel primers have already been published, one of them being "The Story of the Cross."

3. The need to engage multitudes of individuals in the task of teaching. The movement has adopted as its slogan, "Each one teach one." The hope is that each

---

[1] "Like Trying To Tear Down the Himalayas," *The Missionary Herald*, July, 1937, p. 283.

adult pupil, after receiving a lesson, will go and teach it to two friends before he comes for his second lesson.

4. The need for enlisting the aid of students in this effort. A few schools and colleges have already entered upon this form of vacation service; and in some cases during term time the school or college servants are taught. At the last meeting of the Board of Governors of Isabella Thoburn College, Lucknow, perhaps the most interesting feature of the day was a procession of all those in the college compound who had learned to read, together with their teachers.

SANITATION AND HEALTH

Education is not the only need of the village. Sanitation and health, economic uplift, a new attitude toward women, and a new view of God that frees from sin, supersition and fear, are all basic requirements for the redemption of village life. All these needs form a vicious circle. To destroy this circle it must be broken into at as many arcs as possible. When the late Dr. Kenyon L. Butterfield visited India a few years ago, he advocated the establishment by Christian missions of "rural units" that would attack simultaneously at many points the problems of rural reconstruction. An important principle is that changes should come from the cooperation of villagers themselves, and not through external compulsion.

The need for medical help is pressing and most difficult to supply. Illness is rife. Hookworm, guinea worm, malaria, typhoid, cholera, and many other preventable diseases take their toll of efficiency and often of life. Among Christian agencies, various experiments are being tried. In some places a doctor camps in a central village, and patients from adjacent villages come daily to the tent-dispensary.

ECONOMIC UPLIFT

Another pressing need is that for economic improvement. Much enlightenment on this subject has come from the investigations of Dr. and Mrs. William H. Wiser of the North India Presbyterian Mission. For five successive cold seasons they and their two little sons lived in tents on the outskirts of a typical North India village, to which they have given the fictitious name of Karimpur. In a book called *Behind Mud Walls*,[1] Dr. and Mrs. Wiser have given a fascinating and intimate account of the life of the twenty-four castes that live as a complete unit or "commune" in that village organization. Through five years of friendship based on medical service and the give and take of daily intercourse, the Wiser family became friends with Brahmans and Sweepers alike, and were given close-up views of the self-contained social and economic structure into which the castes of a village of some seven hundred souls are

----

[1] New York, Harper & Brothers, 1930.

welded. In a recent book[1] Dr. Wiser has explained with scientific accuracy the complicated system of service and privilege which through two thousand years has been built into the caste system of Indian life. It is a system of wonderful complexity which insures against unemployment and insecurity and prevents individualism by subordinating the individual entirely to the service of his family, caste and village. Each member of a caste serves the community and in turn is served by it. For example, the potter provides the village with clay water-jars and cooking vessels, and in return is served by the priest, the washerman, the water carrier, the tailor, the carpenter, and the scavenger. Most of this work is carried on without money transaction, remuneration being provided either by exchange of service or by payments in kind, such as grain or other kinds of food. There is much in the system that India needs to retain, and much that western civilization might well envy. The chief counts against it are its discouragement of personal initiative, and the inflexibility which prevents an able and gifted person born in an Untouchable caste from improving his condition or rising to a position of leadership.

AGRICULTURAL SCHOOLS

Workers for economic improvement have two prime purposes. The first is the reform of agriculture through

[1] W. H. Wiser, *The Hindu Jajmani System*, Section I. Lucknow Publishing House, Lucknow, India, 1936.

the introduction of better animals, better seed, better agricultural implements, and more diversified crops. To further this ideal, Christian missions have founded agricultural schools in various parts of the country.

An interesting piece of extension work is done by the Sangli Movable School. This consists of a Ford 1½ ton truck with commodious body in which is carried almost every conceivable article useful for village uplift work. There are illustrated charts and posters, touching upon phases of village life; there is a traveling dispensary; there is a circulating library; a crate or two of chickens and a couple of good milk goats have a stall in the truck. That commodious body and those charts and posters are Sangli-made. There are all kinds of seed samples for field and garden crops. Then this Movable School has its own portable generating unit, also stereopticon and 16mm movie projector. At night the surroundings are lit up like fairy-land, and there have been as many as 3,500 people sitting out in the open for the illustrated lectures. What opportunities for reaching needy people through eye-gate and ear-gate! The program of this Movable School aims to touch every phase of rural life. Bible classes have been conducted for the men of the village as early as five A.M. Frequently the middle-aged will assemble at dusk for their classes in reading and writing, for the School is carrying on a campaign against illiteracy. There are special days for the women and children. The Indian crew consists of three fine Christian leaders. "Serve and save the village" is their motto.[1]

The Katpadi Institute in the south includes a higher elementary school in which Christian boys, largely of village origin, combine the ordinary school course with all the outdoor activities of a farm. Such boys leave school with a new and wholesome attitude toward manual labor; they look upon it with respect because they and their teachers together have done such work under favorable and happy conditions; to them farm work is no longer the degrading bondage of a serf but a vocation requiring intelligence and producing satisfaction in the worker.

COTTAGE INDUSTRIES

But not even improvements in agriculture—making two blades of wheat or rice grow where one grew before —will prevent seasonal unemployment and idleness, with resultant poverty. To overcome this there must be a revival of the cottage industries that flourished in India before the days of the industrial revolution and the world-wide relations of trade and commerce that resulted from it. It is for this purpose that Mr. Gandhi so passionately advocates the revival of cotton spinning in every village home. This which has been described as the "most talked-about cottage vocation" brings in a

[1] "The Supreme Interest of India," by John L. Goheen, in *The Presbyterian Tribune*, August 6, 1936.

mere pittance a day, yet that very pittance may ward off starvation. Or, if the thread is not sold, it may be woven into cloth sufficient to clothe the family. In India, just as the automobile and the bullock cart run side by side along the same road, so the great cotton mills and the primitive looms work in close proximity; and in both cases collisions are less frequent than we might expect. The wearing of *khaddar,* that is, cloth woven from homespun thread, has been one of the planks of the Indian National Congress. Good *khaddar* is a little more expensive than mill cloth, but it is worn as a patriotic symbol by thousands of Nationalists, and in spite of its coarseness has a dignity and beauty of its own. *Khaddar* sales have been large enough to make serious inroads upon the consumption of foreign cloth and to increase unemployment in Lancashire.

In Christian circles there has been less emphasis upon spinning and more upon a diversified program of cottage industries. Dr. Spencer Hatch, who has organized an outstanding piece of rural reconstruction in the Indian state of Travancore, has found it possible to further such industries as hand-loom weaving, poultry raising, bee-keeping, palm-sugar making, and the cultivation of the cashew nut, all of them indigenous industries needing further development.

COOPERATIVE MARKETING

Dr. Hatch soon discovered that production is not enough; the marketing of the product is imperative. "I have seen rural people very puzzled and discouraged when they have learned to produce a better commodity, but have not found a market that would pay the higher price the better commodity was worth."[1] So from production this organization has gone on to cooperative marketing, organized entirely on the basis of self-help associations. These successful efforts are revolutionizing the rural life of this section of Travancore.

In Katpadi a small building has been rented as a center for the marketing of improved eggs. There the villager, Christian or non-Christian, may bring the product of his improved poultry yard. At the agricultural farm he has learned to construct simple but efficient poultry runs; to substitute good breeds of poultry for country stock; to feed and care for his birds in a scientific manner. This egg center enables him to ship eggs of a size that amaze the villager, and to receive an adequate price in return, with no exaction from the middleman. As the villager goes into the egg center it is with the honest pride of a good farmer that he sees his eggs weighed, dated and placed in rows with hundreds of others that are to be skillfully packed and shipped by rail to the great city a hundred miles away.

AN INDIAN CHRISTIAN VILLAGE

For a brighter side of the picture, I turn to the memory of a South Indian Christian village, which I have

---

[1] D. Spencer Hatch, *Up from Poverty in Rural India*, p. 17. New York, Oxford University Press, 1936.

known since my earliest years in India. This village was
at that time seven miles from the nearest railway station;
a few years ago a new station was opened not more than
four miles distant. It is still seven miles from the nearest
town and weekly market. It is not on the main road but
can be approached only by negotiating a mile or two of
cart track across waste lands and dry cultivation fields.
Many years ago the majority of the outcaste section of
this large village became Christian. These outcastes
were neither Sweepers nor Chamars, but Pariahs. This
term, which has been adopted into English as a synonym
for a social outcaste whether canine or human, really de-
notes an Untouchable Tamil caste one or two steps
above those of which we have been speaking. This village group was large enough to "come over" without
much social dislocation, and proved particularly respon-
sive to Christian teaching and educational opportunity.

A little church and a tiny school were built early in its
history. The former has been replaced by a commodious
building suited to the growing congregation; for its
erection money was collected and saved over a long
period of years. The school also grew from a one-
teacher to a three-teacher school. Boys and girls went
away to boarding school, to high school, to college and
theological seminary. A large number of catechists,
pastors, and teachers have been drawn from this village
of Yehamur. Undoubtedly this has been bad for the village for its best blood has been drawn away. The miti-

gating circumstance is the fact that in this case there
has been no dislocation. Children who earn have sent
back money to parents, for the purchase of land and the
building of better houses. For holidays and funerals,
for weddings and festivals, children and grandchildren
come home; their roots are still in the village and their
pride is in it too. I think of a Christian catechist of
small education who went out from Yehamur. Out of
his large family of children several sons are college
graduates, two are pastors, and one a teacher in a
normal training school. One daughter has successfully
completed her medical course and is now an interne in
the hospital of the Vellore Medical College. The father
has retired, and his sons have built him a comfortable
house in the village, neat, sanitary and attractive. The
aged father and mother make this their home and it is
the center to which the educated sons and daughters return for holidays and all special occasions.

Uplift of Rural Women

A further need, and an urgent one, is the uplift of
village women. The disabilities of rural women are in
some way similar to those of their town-bred sisters, in
other ways quite different. The system of *purdah,* or the
seclusion of women, varies widely in the various areas
of the Indian subcontinent. In general, there is less of it
in villages than in towns and cities.

But though most village women escape the curse of

seclusion they suffer from many other disabilities—long hours of unrelieved toil at the grinding of grain, the making of cow-dung cakes for fuel, the carrying of the heavy waterpot, the cooking of food over a smoky and chimneyless fire through months of grilling heat, as well as long hours of back-breaking toil in rice field or during the wheat harvest. Joined with this are the evils of early marriage, too frequent bearing of children, high death rate due to undernourishment, complete ignorance of sanitation, and lack of medical aid. Utter ignorance and a heavy load of superstition complete the picture.

Until the women of the village are freed from these burdens, there is no hope for uplifting the rural community. Mr. F. L. Brayne, the chief Government exponent of rural reconstruction in the Punjab, has said, 'Educate a boy and you uplift an individual; educate a girl and you uplift a whole family." It is only as men and women advance equally, that family and community life can change. Any program that forgets the women of a village is too short-sighted to survive.

THE NEED OF CHRISTIAN FAITH

The last great need of the village is for a new type of religious faith, without which the motive power for reform will be lacking. Yet such faith must be imparted, not in a social vacuum, but with and through such tangible help as quinine, latrines, marketing facilities, pri-

mary schools, cooperatives, ventilation, village news-
papers, better seed, wells.

. A new religious faith is needed for the removal of
superstition and its attendant fears. Anyone who knows
even a little of the psychology of the villager will find
new meaning in the biblical statement that "fear hath
torment" and that only "perfect love casteth out fear."
There has been little conscious effort on the part of ex-
ponents of the higher forms of Hinduism to impart its
more spiritual teachings to the uneducated. Hence the
village pantheon is formed of the ancient animistic gods
that have arisen out of a nature worship of vast antiq-
uity. These, unlike the bright gods of Greece, usually
symbolize the dark and fearful powers of nature, and
naturally so, for a tropical and sub-tropical country subject to burning heat, to alternations of flood and famine,
to poverty and pestilence, shows to its poorer children
little of the kindlier forms of nature. And so rites of
propitiation are paid to the deadly but sacred cobra, to
goddesses of cholera and smallpox, to demons that
dwell in the *neem* tree with its fragrant blossoms and
bitter medicinal leaves, to ghosts that haunt the deep
well of the suicide and the burning ghat. Under a tree
one finds two or three rough stones smeared with ver-
million paint and sacred *ghi,* a little garland of jasmine
and oleander, a broken cocoanut, sometimes the blood
of a cock. When the scourge of cholera walks abroad
in the land, then nightly processions go forth with beat

of tom-tom and shout of fear to lead or drive the spirit
of pestilence outside the limits of the village.

As it was in the Europe of the Dark and even the
Middle Ages, so here it needs more than two or three
generations of Christian teaching to dispel these ancient
fears through faith in the protecting care of an all-
powerful and loving God. I have found it quite useless
to attempt to prove that there is no devil pouncing from
the dark branches of the *neem* tree; no spirit lying in
wait beside the unused well; it is far more effective to
urge that God is stronger than the devil, and that

> "From ghosties and ghoulies
> And ill-favored beasties,
> And things that go bump
>   in the night"

the good Lord can deliver us.

Striking Results in Leadership

Already leaders of force and ability have emerged
from the rural life of India, among non-Christians as
well as Christians. Many of the former have come from
the higher castes, as for example the two Patel brothers
and other well known names in Congress circles. Here
and there, too, throughout the centuries, men of influence have arisen out of the depressed classes themselves.
In Travancore one such, Sri Narayana Guru, has recently been the acknowledged spiritual leader of one of
the greatest depressed communities of that state.

A few years ago in South India I had the privilege of seeing an outstanding piece of village uplift work, which was carried on without any money contribution from outside the village itself. Roads had been repaired, pits filled up, waste land reclaimed, latrines built, houses put in order, until the village was a changed place to live in. All this had been done by local unpaid labor, each household being assessed for one day's work each month by each man in the family. The men of the village met in assembly on the night of each new-moon-day, and planned the project which they would take up for the coming month. All this was due to the voluntary leadership of an educated member of the village, a landlord who had caught the vision of a better life for his co-landowners and tenants, both caste and outcaste. The rise of such local unpaid leadership in every village would spell the social salvation of rural India.

From among village Christians of depressed class origin, leadership of another type has emerged. Among the outcastes there is always a proportion of children who prove capable of receiving higher education and of profiting by it. Intelligence testing has not yet been sufficiently perfected in India to prove just what that proportion is; we only know that it exists. In my own experience I have known the children of illiterate parents in outcaste villages who in the first generation of education have completed a high school course through the medium of English—a completely foreign language never spoken or heard in the village environment. I have known girls of similar origin whose parents had received an elementary education, who have gone straight through a medical school or arts college. They have come out to fulfill successfully the duties of a doctor, a head mistress, a school inspectress, or a Student Christian Movement secretary, holding positions of influence among those of higher birth and better economic opportunity than themselves. Some of our finest Christian pastors, possessed of both mental ability and spiritual power, have risen from the same lowly origin. Vast reservoirs of potential power for the renewal of India's life can be released from these underprivileged masses. Every Christian school that ministers to humble village folk is helping to unlock that reservoir.

CHAPTER IV

THE MINISTRY OF HEALING IN INDIA

By B. CHONÉ OLIVER, M.D. and L. B. CARRUTHERS, M.D.

THE SCUDDER MEMORIAL HOSPITAL

IN the afternoon of a warm day in August, 1935, a small group of the Scudder family was gathered together around a newly made grave in front of the lovely white Scudder Memorial Hospital in Ranipet, South India. Silently, reverently they stood in the little triangular plot of grass and ferns that enclosed the flag-draped tombstone of their ancestors, Dr. and Mrs. John Scudder, the first medical missionaries to come to India from America. For nearly a hundred years their bodies had lain in an obscure part of the Christian cemetery in Madras. Their great-grandson and namesake had gone to Madras, received permission to have the bodies disinterred, and had brought the sacred handful of dust and laid it in the new grave in front of the hospital which had been erected as a memorial to Dr. Scudder one hundred years after his arrival in India. Dr. Ida Scudder, founder of Vellore Hospital and Medical School, the only grandchild in India at the time, stepped forward and slowly drew aside the flag, unveiling a large white marble slab. Deeply moved, everyone bent forward to read the inscription:

JOHN SCUDDER—INDIA, 1819-1855
HARRIET WATERBURY SCUDDER—INDIA, 1819-1849

In 1819 the germ theory of disease had not yet been formulated. Anaesthesia for operating was unknown. There was no protection whatever from cholera, malaria, typhoid or smallpox. And yet this young couple had the divine courage to come to India where they lived and preached and healed the sick for nineteen years before they took their first furlough. Mrs. Scudder raised a family which for four generations has contributed more missionaries to India than any other in the world. By the eloquence of his preaching and even more by the beauty and unselfishness of his life, Dr. Scudder won large numbers of Indian people to Christ. He successfully performed major surgical operations in his own home under conditions that would be regarded as impossible today. He walked unharmed among the stricken people during cholera and smallpox epidemics, administering to them the best available remedies of the time. Incredible as this seems, yet even more incredible is the result of his thirty-six years in India. The large, modern Scudder Memorial Hospital in Ranipet is one of over two hundred and fifty-six mission hospitals now scattered throughout the whole of India. And today three hundred and fifty doctors and three hundred nurses are carrying on the medical missionary work he began only a little over a hundred years ago.

EARLY WOMEN DOCTORS

The first woman doctor sent to India was Dr. Clara Swain, who reached Bareilly in 1870, not long after the first women physicians began to practice in America. Miss Elizabeth Bielby soon followed and opened the medical work at Lucknow. In 1881, on the morning of her departure to England, Miss Bielby was visited by the Maharani of Punna, a former patient. "You are going to England," said the royal lady. "I want you to tell the Queen what the women of India suffer when they are sick." She then gave charge that Miss Bielby herself was to convey the message to the Queen. She asked her to write it down. "Write small, Doctor Miss Sahib," she said, "for I want you to put it into a locket and you are to wear this locket around your neck till you see our great Queen and give it to her yourself. You are not to send it through another." Miss Bielby duly reached England, when the Queen, hearing of the message, sent for her and graciously admitted her to a personal interview. To what Miss Bielby said of the condition of suffering Indian women, Her Majesty listened with much interest, asking many questions, and showing the deepest sympathy. The locket with its writing was given the Queen, and Her Majesty entrusted Miss Bielby with a kind and suitable reply.[1]

This interview was one of the causes of the formation

---

[1] *The Work of Medical Women in India,* by Margaret Balfour and Ruth Young. New York, Oxford University Press, 1929.

of the Countess of Dufferin Fund to render medical aid by women to the women of India. Fifty years ago there were only twenty-four women doctors practicing in India, whereas today there are twenty-six in the Zenana Hospitals of Delhi alone. The government maintains the Women's Medical Service and the close bonds that exist between this service and women medical missionaries is evidenced by the fact that, up to the present, most of the chief medical officers of that service and its college principals have been appointed from among women medical missionaries.

MEDICAL COMPETITION: AMERICA OR INDIA?

"True, I think we are filling a real need here, but fully half my time is taken up convincing the others of the existence of this need." Such was the remark uttered by the medical head of the department of student health in a large American university recently. Advertise so as to convince people of their need for the thing you have to sell, is the watchword of American business. Write articles, be appointed to the staffs of the better hospitals, do research so that your name may be connected with some new discovery or some new method of treatment; these are the ways of "selling oneself" in the medical profession. All this raises a fundamental question. The needs are real, no doubt, but is not the strain of competition forcing exaggerations of them?

"Oh, what is the use? There won't be anybody there,"

replied one young New York doctor when asked why he was not in his office at the time that he had announced as his office hours. In America there is approximately one doctor for every 800 people. In India today there are 30,000 physicians among more than 350,000,000 people, one doctor for every 12,000. This varies from one to every 800 people in Madras city to one to every 35,000 in the Central Provinces. Fully half of these doctors are poorly trained and would not be allowed to practice under American laws. The problem in India is not finding enough patients to keep one busy, it is rather finding enough time to attend adequately to those who come desperately sick. There is no need to spend time in competition with fellow physicians and no need to spend time convincing people of the necessity for health. One million lepers; ten million pulled down physically each day by malaria; one hundred thousand untreated cases of tuberculosis walking the streets of Bombay; hookworm sapping the strength of an otherwise vigorous race; vitamin deficiencies and manifold forms of malnutrition; these are the needs that occupy the medical men of India every moment of their days. The task is far too great for the present medical profession in India to cope with. In Allahabad, a city of 183,914 inhabitants, it is estimated that 80% of the illnesses of the people are still being treated by indigenous *hakims* and *waids* (medicine men) who ply their family trade in the villages, small towns and back streets of the cities, a trade that is based on fear, ignorance and superstition. Of necessity this must remain true as long as scientific medical help remains so inadequate.

GOVERNMENTAL AGENCIES

There is much alms-giving in India, but there is no feeling of responsibility for the sufferings of the nation as a whole by the great majority of Indians. There are a few public-spirited men among the wealthy, particularly from among the Parsee community, who, contrary to the usual custom of the land, give generously to such official or semi-official organizations as the Red Cross Society, the King George Fund for Tuberculosis, and the British Empire Leprosy Relief Association. These organizations are active in their respective fields as far as their rather limited funds will permit. But there are no large hospitals supported by public subscription, no giving by medical practitioners of their time to free clinics and dispensaries without remuneration, no support for public health drives, no Community Chests. These last are distinctly Christian institutions and as such are foreign to India, where exist the doctrines of *karma* or punishment by God for sins committed, and the doctrine of *kismet* or fate. A young Indian prince was asked once by his English tutor what he would do for his poverty-stricken subjects when he ascended his throne. He replied, "I am what I am because of my good deeds in some previous incarnation; they are what they are because they were evil. It is their just punishment. For me to help them would be to go against the will of God."

Government agencies are doing their share of such attempts as are being made to relieve the disease, the malnutrition and the insanitary conditions of this land. In all the cities and many of the larger towns are government hospitals or dispensaries, the larger of which are usually well-equipped. They are staffed by members of the Indian Medical Service which, in the past, has borne a well-deserved reputation for its high professional standards. Its services do not extend into the smaller towns and villages, however, and of these there are about eight hundred thousand. The private practitioners crowd into the cities because here the financial return is larger and the villages go neglected.

The average Indian patient is interested only in the treatment of his disease. He does not understand about the need for accurate diagnosis first. As a consequence he will object usually to paying consultation fees or fees for X-rays or laboratory work. If he can pay at all, he will pay for medicine or for surgical operations. It is a great temptation then for the private practitioner to neglect all attempts at accurate diagnosis and to put his stress on the bottle of medicine which he dispenses himself or upon the need for surgery. The standards he sets for his practice fall accordingly. One wonders sometimes if the Indian villager really appreciates the difference between the charm the village "quack" hands out and the bottle of medicine he so trustingly clutches to his breast. The long row of empty patent medicine bottles that is invariably seen by the Mission doctor when he attends upon a chronic invalid is one of the many pathetic examples of economic waste in this great land.

WIDE-SPREAD MEDICAL MISSIONS

Medical missions in India are spread out over the whole country, from the valleys of the Himalayas in the north to the green fields of Ceylon in the south, from the deserts of Baluchistan in the west to the jungles of Assam and Burma in the east. Along the north-western frontier, at the foot of the passes through the mountains, is a chain of dispensaries that are friendly outposts in this unfriendly area. They render aid to those who every year trek back and forth through these passes between India, Afghanistan and Tibet. In these hospitals on the frontier, one is likely to find, besides the ordinary private and public wards, a caravansary ward like an Eastern inn, where friends and relatives can stay with the patient. Lord Roberts said of the late Dr. Theodore Pennell that he was worth two regiments of soldiers in keeping the peace along that turbulent border. At Quetta Sir Henry Holland has built up a hospital and a reputation that brings ophthalmologists from both England and America to study under him. Dr. Douglas Forman's dispensary work at Allahabad is a model of its kind. In Bihar, among the primitive Santals, where Dr. Ronald Macphail, in succession to his father, carries on an extensive eye clinic, during the "cataract season" patients can be seen camped out in the open with their clothes and cooking pots hanging from the trees.

Dr. T. Howard Somervell, who first came to India as a member of the famous Mount Everest expedition on which Mallory and Irvine lost their lives, works in the extreme south of India. Impressed by the needs he saw while on this expedition, he surrendered a brilliant future in London to take charge of the large mission hospital in Neyyoor. This hospital is noted for its development of small, out-lying hospitals, some of which are over one hundred miles from the large central one. In this way the institution is able to serve an enormous community and to treat over 150,000 patients yearly. At Miraj, in western India, through the efforts of Sir William Wanless and Dr. Charles Vail, there has been built up the largest of these medical missionary hospitals of India, an institution that includes a large general hospital, a medical school and nursing school and both leper and tuberculosis sanatoria. These larger general mission hospitals are usually fairly well equipped and adequately staffed, although not sufficiently so as to permit the critical observation of patients which is routine in American hospitals of the same size.

This, however, cannot be said of the smaller mission hospitals. What they lack along these lines, they attempt to make up by self-sacrificing care of their patients. In the capital city of one of the larger Indian states, there is one of these small, poorly equipped mission hospitals and a much larger, beautifully equipped and well staffed government hospital. The former is nearly 100% full every day, the latter rarely more than 20% so. Asked why this was, a leading Brahman citizen of that city replied, "Because people know that in the mission hospital they will be cared for and seen every day, whereas in the government hospital they may lie four or five days at a time without once being visited by a doctor."

ZENANA HOSPITALS

Half the mission hospitals of India are staffed by women doctors. Because of the religious and social customs of both Islam and Hinduism, these *"zenana* hospitals," as they are popularly called, are restricted to the treatment of women and children. This is particularly so in the north of India. One of the finest examples of this type of hospital is to be found at Lucknow, where the Zenana Bible Mission Hospital has for years given practically the only medical aid open to the *purdah*-bound Moslem women of that city. Though always crowded to over-flowing, a man can walk through the wards of this hospital and never see a patient, as each bed is carefully screened off by heavy curtains. In Bombay Presidency, however, the *purdah* system is only uncommonly found and here women patients will come quite freely to male doctors and, conversely, a large proportion of the patients in the *zenana* hospitals, such as the one at Kolhapur, are men.

In one year about 32,000 maternity cases are treated in the mission hospitals of India. Of these, about one third are abnormal. Because of the superstition and religious customs that surround child-bearing, it is difficult in many parts of India to get expectant mothers to come to the hospitals. This feeling is breaking down, however, and already in the city of Bombay it is estimated that 80% of births occur in the hospitals and maternity homes. In the villages and small towns, however, there is still the local *dai* or midwife for attendance on women at childbirth. As childbirth is a time of impurity, the *dai* is always uneducated and of low caste and she has no training for her task beyond that of her own experience. Since the bed and bedding are frequently burned after the birth or given to the *dai,* only the oldest things are used, and the worst room in the home is the lying-in chamber. These women have no idea of the mechanism of birth or of asepsis. In any difficulty their only remedy is force, often applied with disastrous consequences.

Women who have always lived in *purdah* are often great sufferers at childbirth because of their lack of sunshine, fresh air and exercise. They are prone to anemia, to tuberculosis, or to adult rickets, and this last causes such deformities that the child can often only be born by Caesarian section. It is estimated that 200,000 women die yearly in India at childbirth from preventable causes. In attempts to meet this situation, many of the mission hospitals conduct classes for training these village *dais* and a great many of the Indian Christian nurses are taking up midwifery.

EVANGELISTIC WORK IN HOSPITALS

In all these hospitals, side by side with the treatment of the patients, side by side with the training of the student nurses and patients themselves, goes on the evangelistic work. Sometimes the doctors and nurses do it directly in the morning prayers or the clinic or ward services, sometimes they carry it on only indirectly through the lives they are living. In most hospitals there are also official hospital evangelists who are usually Indian and who sometimes are highly qualified. Usually there is some one in each hospital who makes it his job to distribute magazines and other reading material to the bed-ridden patients. The number of those who desire to take the opportunity during their illness to read the New Testament is truly remarkable. The interest of the average Indian in things of the spirit has no parallel in any other country.

In one hospital a nursing sister, who also is the evangelist, tells of a woman who was in a terrible condition, physically, mentally and morally, living in filthiness and subject to wild outbursts of temper. This woman followed the nursing sister into the chapel one morning and there asked to be allowed to help with the dusting. After that she came regularly each day, seeming to find relief in the peaceful atmosphere of the chapel. One day when they were there together, the woman pointed to the black marble cross embedded in the floor and asked what it was. Being told of its meaning she grasped the idea that the chapel was hers and the cross was there for her. Her life began to be different. She took over the work of keeping the chapel clean. She would bathe each day before coming to scrub the floor. When it was suggested that her work should be changed she was afraid and pleaded to be allowed to continue. "You see, sister, Jesus saves me here. I come and look at this cross and I know that I am safe. I never want to leave this work."

HIGHER HEALTH STANDARDS

In the Christian community, where mission medical work can be carried on more effectively, there is most clearly evidenced the result of the impact of better standards of health, cleanliness and medical care upon the people. There caste customs or local superstition are not hampering factors. Epidemics do not mean angry gods that must be appeased, nor does adding chlorine to the water supply simply mean defiling it. The houses of the pastor or teacher in the Christian school are usually models of cleanliness for those living around. Health measures are taught in both the day and Sunday schools. Christian mothers have learned to bring their children to the doctors when they first become sick rather than attempting to treat them at home with patent medicines, and annual physical examinations are routine to many of them. All this has resulted in the infant mortality rate being lower and the life-expectancy rate being longer among the Christians than among the rest of the population of India. The Indian Christian, despite his origin, in the great majority of instances, from the lowest strata of Hindu society, is classified in the Indian Government Census as from the "advanced" communities.

Often the hospital has brought the local Christian church and community into being. There was not a single Christian in Miraj when the late Sir William Wanless first went there in 1889. Today there is a strong, vigorous church of six hundred members. In the central part of India, in a small town, where twenty-five years ago one of the earliest graduates of the Miraj Medical School went to work, today, largely as a result of his effort and example, there is a small church and a Christian community of three hundred.

THE LEPERS OF INDIA

The leper in India is the "cursed of God." The number of these unfortunate people who walk the streets of the cities, begging for alms, uttering their plaintive cries of *"Sahib, Sahib, baksheesh Sahib,"* is one of the disgraces of this great land. The attitude of Hindu society that they are social pariahs, the fact that their disease is scattered through large parts of India and penetrates into the remotest villages, and insufficient finances for the government to tackle so large a problem—these are the reasons for the general neglect of this problem by the official agencies. The British Empire Relief Association has done considerable in giving grants to various hospitals and dispensaries to finance the treatment of lepers in their clinics. Not so many years ago this was considered to be the true solution to the problem, but many question its efficacy now. New understanding of the ways in which the disease spreads and a fuller realization of the relative ineffectiveness of chaulmoogra oil of which so much was expected, has led to this change in attitude. It is now believed that only in the leper sanatoria can cures be effected. From these sanatoria patients are being discharged as cured or at least arrested. Such can not be said for the treatment given to these people as patients in the various out-patient clinics. In the sanatorium, the leper receives rest, good food and fresh air and all his surroundings are improved hygienically. It would seem that these are as fundamental in the treatment of leprosy as they are in tuberculosis. Here also, as he improves, he is permitted to do some work and so to help support himself and his family. At the same time he is kept from infecting others, particularly the children who are so susceptible to this disease.

As he comes down from one of the hill stations near

Bombay, the traveler by bus makes his first stop in a little town that nestles in the valley below. As the bus slows down in the market-place, from the surrounding buildings and the near-by alleys come lepers to beg from the passengers, hobbling along on their crippled feet, holding out their deformed hands. Some of the lepers are young boys and girls, some are mothers with little children clinging to their skirts and oblivious to the fact that most certainly they are passing on their dread disease to these little ones. From time to time they are advised by some responsible person where they can receive treatment but they never heed, ignorant of or ignoring the fact that they are a menace to those around, intent only on the few pennies their condition can induce the travelers to give.

Not so many miles from that little town is one of the Homes of the Mission to Lepers. Its neat, white-washed buildings, grouped around the central chapel, are surrounded by flower gardens and shaded by great banyan trees. Here in little rooms, each with its own house-keeping facilities, live the leper in-patients receiving their treatments regularly. Each day their wounds are properly dressed. Each day they receive the good food that they require. Each day they spend working in the near-by fields, keeping the grounds neat, caring for the gardens or taking part in the many educational activities of the Home. They have their own self-government organization. They have their little evangelistic band also that goes out into the bazaars of the surrounding villages to sing and to tell the story of Christ. A year or so ago, the Governor of Bombay visited the town where that leper home is located and of all the many things he saw, what impressed him most was the play that the lepers wrote, staged and acted in his honour.

In 1930, two hundred and forty-two lepers were discharged as symptom-free from the homes of the Mission to Lepers. In 1935 this number rose to nine hundred and twenty. At Chingleput, south of Madras, is the largest of these leper sanatoria under the care of Dr. Cochrane, who has given his life to the study of this one disease. In the Central Provinces, the Mission to Lepers has recently developed a farm colony of six thousand acres upon which discharged patients will be settled. No greater joy can be witnessed anywhere than that which comes to these people who, saved from social ostracism and from condemnation to a slowly advancing death, are thus enabled to return, symptom-free, to normal living conditions. The example of Christ is surely being followed in the treatment of leprosy, but the number of lepers in India is great and the sanatoria are few.

TREATMENT OF TUBERCULOSIS

There are nine mission hospitals in India devoted exclusively to the treatment of tuberculosis. This disease, due to poor nutrition of the Indian people and to the crowded, unsanitary conditions under which they live, is very prevalent. Yet in the whole of India there are only four thousand beds available in the different hospitals for its treatment, fewer than are found in some single American cities. Many of these beds are in the nine mission tuberculosis hospitals. The largest tuberculosis sanatorium in India is the Union Mission Tuberculosis Sanatorium at Arogyavaram in South India. Here there are two hundred and thirty-three beds under the care of Dr. C. Frimodt-Möller and his Indian associates. Not only is good modern treatment carried out at Arogyavaram but also government and mission doctors receive post-graduate training. The second largest sanatorium is another union mission project, the Wanless Union Tuberculosis Sanatorium at Miraj. A third large mission sanatorium is being built up with partial government aid, at Pendra Road in the Central Provinces. The long nursing care required for tuberculosis patients and the dread which so many people have of coming into contact with the disease, make ministry to them a task peculiarly appropriate for the Christian doctor and nurse. One of the leading experts on tuberculosis in India today is an Indian Christian doctor at Arogyavaram.

MEDICAL PIONEERING

The days of physical pioneering have practically gone. There are areas up in the mountains of Bombay Province where there are no roads, only foot paths leading through the dense jungle, and where wounds inflicted by wild animals are some of the commonest reasons for consulting the medical man. Most of India is accessible by railway or by gravel road today and the need for opening new country with all its attendant hardships is now almost gone. But there are other great fields open to the pioneering medical missionary. A member of one of the large American mission boards said that he believes every mission institution should be reaching out for better and easier ways of doing its work, new ways of educating its students, new ways of teaching health, new ways of bringing modern medicine to the villager. Many examples of this sort of pioneering are be found. The attempts of some missionary nurses to develop in the villages a modified form of public health nursing is one example, and another is the work of the roadside clinics developed by Dr. Ida Scudder at Vellore, where motors fitted up as traveling dispensaries are sent out daily along advertised routes.

PUBLIC HEALTH CAMPAIGNS

It is, however, in the field of preventive medicine and sanitation that the great opportunity of the future lies. The dean of a large mid-western medical college, while on a visit to India, remarked one day that he had never seen a case of guinea worm, a parasitic disease contracted by drinking infected water. He was taken to a small isolated village some miles away and there in an afternoon he saw over one hundred cases of the disease in all its stages. Two-thirds of the people of that village were infected, but there was not a single case in its large Christian community. Some months previously a missionary had come to the village and had persuaded the Christian people to cover up their well and to use a pump to obtain the water. In this way infected persons were prevented from wading into the water of that well and so spreading the disease. In the next few months the disease died out completely from among the Christians of that village, and in a short while others were asking how they too could rid themselves of the parasite. Such a simple demonstration is worth months of propaganda.

Simple public health campaigns such as this are being conducted all over India, very often by the non-medical missionary. Despite the great opportunities that lie in this field, there is not a single medical missionary in India today who devotes anything but a small proportion of his time to public health. It is one of the great opportunities of the future and one that offers many ways of pioneering in conjunction with the newer developments of village uplift work. A mere repetition of the work that government institutions are doing and doing satisfactorily is not enough; in everything undertaken the mission must blaze new trails.

THE NURSING PROFESSION

In India the nursing profession is 90% Christian. This has been due largely to the confining restrictions with which Islam surrounds its women and to the barriers of caste among the Hindus. However there are signs that a few of the more progressive young Moslem and Hindu women are beginning to think seriously of following their Christian sisters into this great profession. The government hospitals of India have trained many nurses but these have been mostly from the Anglo-Indian community. Most of the native Indian nurses receive their training in mission institutions and many of them have remained in mission work after their graduation. The standards of nursing in India are rapidly rising. Governmental regulation is setting these standards at higher and higher levels, being influenced largely by an increasing national pride and a desire for reciprocity agreements with other countries, notably Great Britain. In many nursing schools, high school graduation is already being required for admission. The mission schools must be prepared not only to meet these rising standards, but also to continue to blaze new trails in nursing education if they are to keep the leadership they have held so long. These rising standards still manifest themselves mostly in the cities and towns. In many places, particularly in the native Indian states, the nursing service in the government hospitals leaves much to be desired or is conspicuous by its absence.

Not long ago the secretary of the Christian Medical Association visited a mission hospital of seventy beds in a large native state. It was rather poorly housed in an old bungalow with some outside wards, but its beds were full, and there was a nurses' training school under a missionary nurse. Across the road was a fine state hospital with two well qualified doctors, a man and a woman, but few patients, and the only nurse on the women's wards was an *ayah,* a practical nurse with no special training whatever.

THE NEED FOR ADEQUATE MEDICAL TRAINING

In the field of the training of physicians and surgeons, the initiative in the past has rested with the governmental medical colleges and schools. Nearly all the eleven Indian provinces have medical colleges in connection with their universities and two or more of the lower grade medical schools. Spurred on by the same influences that are at work in the nursing profession, standards in medical education are rising also and within the next few years the differences now existing between the medical college and the medical school will be abolished. Already new standards set in Bombay for medical schools require two years of pre-medical study in a liberal arts college and four years in medicine, only one year less than in the medical colleges. In Madras the lower grade schools are being abolished altogether. The situation is quite analogous with that facing the nursing schools. If anything, however, it is more acute.

There is still need for great pioneers in the field of Christian medical education in India. At present there are only three mission medical schools in the whole country, all of them lower than college grade: Ludhiana and Vellore for women and Miraj for men. All of these schools are working under great financial handicaps.

The mission medical schools in India have not been above criticism. Over-crowding of classes, inadequate equipment, poorly qualified teaching, staffs overworked with a multiplicity of duties which make impossible that degree of professional excellence which will serve as a stimulus to the students before and after graduation— these are faults more or less true of all three schools. Their staffs, their governing bodies and the Christian Medical Association of India are all keenly aware of these faults. Vellore has already declared its intention of advancing to the higher grade, going forth in faith despite recurring deficits. The school at Miraj is also exerting every effort to reach a similar standard, though here governmental pressure is not so strong as at Vellore, and a more gradual change may be possible. The Ludhiana school receives government aid and there the situation is at present less acute.

The medical missionary of the future must be more willing to hand over greater and greater responsibilities to his Indian associates. In the past it has been felt that the Indian assistant doctors were not sufficiently well trained to take heavy responsibility and that they have not been able to command the confidence of their fellow countrymen. Both of these facts have been true. However the deficiencies in training, of which lack of confidence is a by-product, have not been the fault of the Indians but of the mission medical schools and of the medical missionaries with whom they have subsequently worked.

Too often the medical missionary is kept so busy that he has no time to give to the training of his Indian assistants, thereby being forced to neglect one of the greatest opportunities he has of being of help to India and of inculcating the high ideals and standards of efficiency of Christian medicine. All medical missionaries have not yet learned to look upon their Indian professional associates and say, "He must increase but I must decrease."

Those medical missionaries who have insisted on having time to train their Indian assistants have been rewarded by having men ready and fit to step in at a moment's notice when emergencies occur. One such emergency arose recently in one of the larger mission hospitals of central India when the medical missionary had to return suddenly to America for reasons of health. His young Indian assistant, a graduate of one of the mission medical schools, has carried on in his absence quite successfully and with the full confidence of the patients.

In conversation with the medical head of one of the best known American tuberculosis sanatoria, the name of Dr. Frimodt-Möller was mentioned. "Yes, I know him. He is the man who, out there in India, insists that all his medical assistants be well trained," was the only comment this superintendent made. A large mission eye hospital near Madras has been for years in charge of a mission medical school graduate. In western India, recently, a graduate of the same school went to the mission during the height of the financial depression and offered to assume full financial responsibility for the little branch hospital of which he was in charge. The offer was accepted and today, under a managing committee appointed from that little Christian church of only one hundred and twenty-five members, that hospital is flourishing. A maternity wing and a new assistant doctor have had to be added. The Christian patients take pride in paying for the services they receive in order that poor Hindus and Moslems, many of them better able to pay than they, can be treated free. This last is a sterling example of one of the developments in medical missions to which we look forward.

Not only must the medical missionary in the future devote more time to the training and professional development of his Indian assistants, but also both medical and nursing schools must be prepared to give their students more adequate training in their undergraduate courses. In this education of Christian doctors and nurses a heavy responsibility is devolving upon the missions in India.

INDIAN CHRISTIAN DOCTORS

Despite the deficiencies of the mission schools, their graduates have made notable contributions to the cause of medicine in India. Hundreds of doctors have been trained for mission service. Some have gone into government work and others into private practice. Of those who have entered private practice nearly all have gone into the smaller towns and villages where the need is greatest. Just recently a graduate of one of these schools, who, after post-graduate study in America, built up a prosperous practice in one of the larger towns of India, entered the Indian church as a national missionary, taking his own savings to build a hospital among the people of a desperately needy area.

Another student from a high-caste Hindu family accepted Christ and was baptized after his graduation from medical school. He completed his interneship and then was offered the opportunity to open a dispensary in a little village. His salary was to be fifteen dollars monthly in such months as the financially impoverished mission could pay it. Much more tempting offers failed to move him from his purpose.

Contrast with that the story of a Christian lad who graduated from the best of the government medical colleges and who wanted desperately to enter mission service. Because of a debt incurred for his education at the expensive government college, however, his family forced him to accept employment by an industrial firm at a higher salary than the mission could give him.

Scattered through the towns and villages of India, in charge of dispensaries or smaller hospitals or acting as assistants in larger ones, here and there in charge of large hospitals, here and there in private practice, are found the graduates of our mission schools, practicing their profession in accordance with the highest Christian ethics, being active in their churches and leaders in their communities.

RESPONSIBILITY OF MEDICAL MISSIONS

Speaking of the rapid Indianization of government medical services, the surgeon-general of one of the premier provinces remarked that the responsibility of maintaining the high ideals and scientific methods of western medicine would have to be carried more and more by medical missions. This means that the medical missionary of the future must be of the best that western medicine can produce. A higher and higher calibre and a better and still better training must be demanded of him before he goes to the field. Otherwise he cannot serve as a stimulus to his Indian colleagues.

It also means that the medical and nursing schools of the missions must have an increasingly high standard. The Christian Medical Association of India, which embraces all medical missionaries and most Indian Christian doctors, has put itself on record as favoring the establishment of a medical college of the highest grade and a permanent committee is at work on this project.

H. R. Ferger

PATIENTS ARRIVING AT THE HOSPITAL, KASGANJ, INDIA

THE GENERAL WARD (interior) THE UNION MISSION TUBERCULOSIS SANITORIUM, ARROGYAVARM. IN SOUTH INDIA

The cost of such an institution, both to establish and to maintain, would of necessity be great. The need for it, however, can be readily realized when one remembers the increasing governmental standards for medical practice, the lack of stress on adequate ethical standards in the governmental medical colleges, the relatively high cost of attending these colleges and the need for well trained Indian Christian doctors in mission hospitals and in private village practice. The highest government medical officials have expressed their desire to see such a mission college established and it remains as one of the great projects for the near future. The original plan of building such a college *de novo* because of the cost would at the present not seem feasible. Its more gradual development upon the basis of one of the already-existing medical schools would seem more likely, and more desirable. Too much time, however, must not be allowed to pass.

WIDE OPPORTUNITIES

The associate surgeon in the best known mission eye hospital in India was once a poor outcaste boy. When he was playing in the streets of his native village, an ox-cart came clattering by and struck him and the huge wooden wheel of the overly laden cart passed over his ankle. He was carried to his home and his ignorant parents called in the local *waid,* but in a few days his leg was gangrenous. A Christian Bible woman came by and induced the parents to send the boy to the mission hospital. He was so desperately ill that his leg had to be be amputated and he took months to regain his strength. When he was well again, his parents allowed him to attend the mission schools and there, in the course of time, he passed his high school graduation examinations and entered the medical school at Miraj. During his school career he accepted Christianity. Today he is one of the most influential and loved members of the staff of that hospital and of his community.

This story is not unique nor is it even an unusual one. It is typical of one of the finest effects of medical missions in India. Should a Christian medical college be developed, it would mean the giving of even greater influence to such men in their community, opening for them wider opportunities for service in their towns or villages, or enabling them to accept key positions in the medical profession all over the country, thus showing to the whole of India those ethical standards and that love for the patient which Christ alone can give to those who practice the art of healing.

CHAPTER V

HIGHER CHRISTIAN EDUCATION
IN INDIA

By C. HERBERT and MARY C. RICE

CHRISTIAN MISSIONS AND EDUCATIONAL PIONEERING

TRY to picture for yourselves the educational position in India in the early years of the last century. Hindu learning was confined to the priestly Brahman caste and was transmitted through the medium of an ancient sacred language, the Sanscrit, in temple schools. It concerned itself with the philosophy and literature of the Brahmanical religion. Moslem learning was likewise confined to the study of Arabic and Persian classics, and while more democratic than the Hindu, it was also essentially concerned with abstract and theological subjects. Both systems largely ignored the education of women; neither had come under the influence of modern thought movements; in neither had the vernacular languages been given any importance as sources or media of education; and neither had employed the printing press as a means to extend knowledge amongst the people. The vast majority of the people were entirely illiterate. This does not mean that they were wholly ignorant or uncultured. There are elaborate structures of common thought, tradition, and ceremony possible without a literary education. There are the cultural influences of music, folk drama, folklore and the civilizing usages of highly developed language and social convention. But if we think of education as a means of acquainting all the people with the history of the past and with the facts and principles of life, and of furnishing them with new ideas and purposes for daily needs in a developing world, India was at that time without any education and without any means of securing it.

The early missionaries had therefore to begin from the ground up. There were government officials in Madras, Bengal and Bombay who were grappling with the problem. Public-spirited Indians, such as Rajah Ram Mohan Roy of Bengal, also felt the need for western learning and founded schools for its propagation. But the greatest names in the history of modern education in India are undoubtedly those of William Carey and Alexander Duff, who were missionaries in Calcutta at the time of which we are writing. The Christian institutions, which they founded for the teaching of western learning through the medium of English, represented a far-reaching conviction on the part of their founders that the dissemination of modern scientific ideas and the ideas at the base of western culture were a necessary prelude to the breaking up of the Hindu system and to the reception of Christian truth.

Beginnings of an Educational System

Christian missions begin with preaching and healing. The necessity arises at once for breaking down ignorance and prejudice in the community. This is done by means of schools which create an atmosphere in which the ideas of Christianity may receive an intelligent reception. Christian children must know how to read, else the Bible itself is a closed book to them. The people at large must know how to read and must have the Bible and other Christian literature available in their own speech. And if the Christian church is to have a trained leadership, Christian high schools and colleges are naturally and inevitably the next step.

The record of the founding of the Christian schools of India is an inspiring story of pioneer efforts to fight illiteracy and superstition; to introduce the dynamite of modern knowledge; to provide intellectual training for the children of illiterate Christian converts; to provide the opportunity of Christian education and character training for the children of liberally minded non-Christians; to provide training in trades and crafts for Christian boys; to study and attack the problems of poverty and disease; to prepare students for the high callings of the ministry, teaching and public service. Every one of our Christian schools goes back to some crying need and the response of some person who could see and feel it and was prepared to spend himself in meeting it.

EDUCATIONAL PIONEERS

Christian education has always been a pioneering enterprise. The time was when Christian schools, being the first in the field, were responsible for a very considerable part of the educational work of the country. Even up to very recent years this has been true with respect to the education of girls. But as the government system has developed, and private agencies have undertaken more and more to provide schools for their own children, the function of Christian schools has become more specific. They still have their fundamental importance in relation to the growing Christian church. They still have the opportunity of demonstrating the value of scientific and progressive method. They still exert incalculable influence in the training of hundreds of sterling and able men for the public services; it is doubtful, for example, whether any government or private institution in India has left so great a mark upon the leading men of a great province as the Madras Christian College has done. They still find new fields in technical education, such as chemical engineering at Forman Christian College, Lahore, agricultural teaching and research at Allahabad, physical education at Madras and Lucknow, training for social welfare workers at Bombay, and the training of Christian teachers at several centers. They have always been "schools with a message." Even where they have had to conform to rather rigid curricula and examinations within the government system, Christian educators have always had the opportunity to participate in the councils of the Department of Public Instruction; they have always had opportunity to experiment and to demonstrate a better way; they have always been free to exemplify that difference, that peculiar quality, known as Christian.

HIGHER CHRISTIAN EDUCATION IN INDIA TODAY

Each of the eleven provinces of British India and many of the great Indian states have now a highly organized department of education. At the head of the department is a Director of Public Instruction, and under him there are various administrative and inspecting officers. Schools and colleges follow a curriculum of secular studies which is prescribed for the entire province, and students are "sent up" for uniform examinations, their certificates and degrees being awarded by the central educational or university authorities. This system has some advantages and some disadvantages for a Christian school or college.

It is an advantage for a graduate to have secured a qualification of recognized value. It is an advantage to have to maintain a high standard of teaching and study under the stimulus of inspection. It is an advantage to have the opportunity to shape or improve the educational system of province or state from within. Many Christian educators have had large influence in fixing the subjects of study and the textbooks which must be followed in an entire province.

The disadvantages are also numerous. There is always the danger that distinctly Christian subjects of study may be crowded into a subordinate place. There is the pressure of increasingly high standards of secular teaching which may overload the teachers of an understaffed and underfinanced institution and affect the quality of its peculiarly Christian activities. There is the pressure and preoccupation of an impersonal examination system. And where Christian schools are in receipt of grants-in-aid from public funds, there is always the possibility that their religious activities may be restricted by government order. It is significant that through the years, in the face of these actual or potential disadvantages, the Christian schools have maintained very high standards of achievement while keeping the daily study of the Bible and Christian truth at the center of their program. They are known everywhere as standing for the proclamation of the truth as it is exemplified in Christ, and the people of India, Hindus and Mohammedans as well as Christians, continue to send their sons and daughters to them in numbers far beyond their capacity to receive.

INDIAN EDUCATIONAL LEADERSHIP

Under the new reformed constitution of the Government of India education is a subject which is entirely within the control of the provincial legislatures. The Minister for Education in each province is chosen from the elected representatives of the people. There are a few British officials still in the educational services but their numbers are rapidly diminishing. This is in line with the accepted policy of the "Indianization of the services."

Entirely parallel to this process in government service is the change in the management and control of Christian institutions. There was a time when almost all Christian schools and colleges were managed by missionary headmasters and principals. This was to be expected in the early days. Today the majority of Christian high schools in India have capable and devoted Indian principals; and a number of the most important Christian colleges are administered by Indians. In fact, the success of any Christian institution must really be measured by the degree in which it has trained able and devoted leaders to take over its control and management. The names of Principal S. K. Datta of Lahore, Principal S. K. Rudra and Principal S. N. Mukerji of Delhi, and Principal S. C. Chatterji of Cawnpore stand amongst the ablest of India's Christian educators. Every Christian college in India today has a number of outstanding Indian Christian gentlemen acting as professors and heads of departments and members of its board of directors or trustees. In the south of India at Alwaye there is the Union Christian College, which was founded by Indian Christians and is entirely staffed and controlled by them. This is one of the most significant and promising ventures of the Indian church.

Christian colleges fall into several types according to their mode of affiliation within the prevailing system. They may be major collegiate institutions at great university centers, as at Lahore, Agra, Calcutta, Madras and Bombay; they may be outlying colleges occupying important territory in provincial cities, as at Rawalpindi and Guntur; they may be units in a federal type of university as at Delhi; or they may be "internal colleges" at government universities such as at Lucknow, where the Isabella Thoburn College for Women is virtually the women's department of the university, or at Allahabad, where the Ewing Christian University College (popularly known as "Holland Hall") and the Agricultural Institute have the unique position of being Christian colleges within a great and prominent government university.

HIGHER CHRISTIAN EDUCATION FOR WOMEN

The Christian church and the Christian home and the Christian school have provided for India's women the greatest awakening and stimulus. Try to imagine the baffling problem presented to early missionaries and Christian leaders by the age-long seclusion of women in the home or behind the veil, and by the prevailing belief that they are essentially inferior, that they must be in subjection, that their only sphere is in the rigidly guarded area of the family, that learning and freedom and public service are not for them. Many influences today are combining to bring about vast and rapid changes in the ideas and practices of Hindu and Mohammedan society with regard to the position of women. Many progressive non-Christian leaders of both sexes are in the forefront of these reform movements, but it must be recognized that Christian missions have had the greatest part in bringing about the new day of enlightenment and liberation. "Until 1857 the education of girls and women was left almost entirely in the hands of Christian missionaries, aided by the courageous revolt of the leaders of progressive thought in religion."[1]

All over India, well into the present century, there was great prejudice against the education of women and much unwillingness on the part of Hindu and Moslem parents to send their daughters to school. For a hundred years there have been Christian schools for Christian boys and girls, as a result of which the proportion of literacy among Christian women is about seven times as great as among the total female population, notwithstanding that five-sixths of all the Christian families in India have come from the lower orders of the social scale.[2] Little by little prejudice was broken down, here and there a few non-Christian parents began to send their daughters to Christian schools, until today we see a general awakening in regard to women's edu-

---

[1] Cornelia Sorabji, in *Our Cause,* edited by S. K. Nehru, p. 4. Allahabad, Kitabistan, 1936.

[2] See Lady Hartog in *Living India,* p. 135.

cation. We must not forget the constant witness that has been given through the years by the Christian homes of India, in which the women and mothers have been free and educated and have taken an active part in the life of the surrounding community; nor the example and influence of the young Christian women who as educated and trained teachers and nurses have shown to India what beautiful and necessary service to society women are able and entitled to give.

NEW EMPHASIS ON EDUCATION OF GIRLS

In every province special officers have been appointed to organize and administer girls' education, and Government and people are giving it new emphasis and attention, although as yet "owing to conservatism, the *purdah* system, and early marriage, the education of girls, in spite of recent advances, is far behind that of boys. . . . . At the primary stage there are four times as many boys as girls; at the middle stage eighteen times as many; at the 'high' stage thirty-four times as many; in the arts colleges there are thirty-three times as many."[1] In other words, the great majority of girls who have been privileged to go to school at all are taken out of school by their parents before they have finished the lower primary classes. This constitutes one of the most serious educational problems.

[1] Sir Philip Hartog, chapter on Education, in *Modern India,* edited by Sir John Cumming. New York, Oxford University Press, 1932.

While government and private agencies are putting special emphasis today upon the extension of girls' education, even now "Christian missions are still making an impressive contribution both in extent of educational facilities and in quality."[1] Forty-four per cent of all girls attending high school in India are enrolled in Christian schools, and more than half of all girls attending college or being trained as teachers are in Christian missionary institutions.[2] The pioneering efforts made by women missionaries may have seemed very small and discouraging, but when we compare them with the volume and rapidity of the women's movement in the East today we thank God for the courage and vision of those devoted women.

EXAMPLES OF CHRISTIAN COLLEGES FOR WOMEN

"Isabella Thoburn College at Lucknow grew out of the boarding school for girls that was established in 1870 by Miss Isabella Thoburn in a mud-walled room in the bazaar. This remarkable woman was the first missionary sent out by the Woman's Foreign Missionary Society of the Methodist Episcopal Church after its organization in 1869. Only one girl came on the opening day, but Miss Thoburn was a woman of unfaltering faith and she was not discouraged. Before her death, Septem-

---

[1] Ruth Francis Woodsmall, *Eastern Women Today and Tomorrow*, pp. 134-135. Boston, Central Committee on the United Study of Foreign Missions, 1933.
[2] Figures quoted from R. Littlehailes, *Progress of Education in India*, Vol. II, 1922-27.

ber 3, 1901, she had seen her little school develop into a college in 1886. In 1919, it became a union college."[1]

Isabella Thoburn College, with its present beautiful plant, its excellent staff of Indian and American Christian teachers, its distinctive Christian atmosphere and influence, is an institution in which the church and missions may take just pride.

The outstanding college for women in South India is the Women's Christian College of Madras. It was opened in 1915 under the auspices of twelve mission boards in Britain, the United States and Canada. In twenty years its growth has been phenomenal. The principal, Dr. Eleanor McDougall, writes:

"The College opened on July 7, 1915, in a rented building called 'Hyde Park' in the southwest region of the city. Though small, it was curiously complete even at the outset. We had all the four university classes, though Class IV consisted of only one member, a student of philosophy. There were ten in the junior B.A. class, seven in the senior intermediate class, and twenty-three beginners. Among these forty-one students there were seven Hindus of various castes, three Anglo-Indians, three Syrian Christians speaking Malayalam, one Kanarese girl, several Telugus, and a majority of Tamil-speaking students, so that we were polyglot from the beginning.

[1] A. J. Brown, *One Hundred Years*, p. 619. New York, Fleming H. Revell Co., 1936.

"The governing body and the staff were already representative of our international, interdenominational and
intercontinental character. We began with a resident
staff of five, of whom one was an Indian graduate of
Madras University, one an American graduate from
Vassar; Oxford, Cambridge and London were represented in the English staff, and the Congregational, Presbyterian and Anglican churches all had adherents among
us.

"Several of our most lasting characteristics were present from the first. Morning and evening prayers were
held daily and a small room, just large enough to hold
the students, the staff and one or two more, was set
apart for our chapel. The Sunday evening services began on our very first Sunday. We had physical drill and
games daily from the first, and one of our earliest subjects for the debating society was the question whether
participation in these should be compulsory. We began
an organization for student self-management, and the
students met on one of our first evenings to choose the
motto and the badge of the College. Also we began on
the first evening of our college life the habit of dining
together, which has proved a very important instru-
ment of our unity."[1]

Through generous donations and through sharing in
the gifts from the West for the "Seven Union Women's

---

[1] Dr. Eleanor McDougall, in *Women's Christian College, Madras, 1915-
1935.*

Colleges in the East," this college now has modern well equipped buildings and a college chapel which is one of the loveliest places for Christian worship in the whole of India. In these twenty years more than a thousand of the finest young women of India have studied in this college and have gone out to share with the people of their country the blessings of their Christian education.

A similar story could be told of the early days of the Kinnaird College for Women at Lahore, which grew out of the Christian Girls' High School of the Zenana Bible and Medical Mission. It had its days of small beginnings. It has received increasingly large classes far beyond capacity since 1919. Kinnaird College has now purchased a large campus outside the crowded city and is ready to enter upon a great day of development if only generous supporters can be found.

Of inestimable value is the great Union Medical College for Women at Vellore, a pioneering venture which today has come to fruition under the inspiring leadership of Dr. Ida Scudder, known to a wide circle of friends of India in the West. The ample campus and great white buildings of that college are an eloquent reminder of the tender and skillful medical and nursing service which its many graduates are rendering to the women and children of India today. In the same connection should be mentioned the Women's Union Hospital and Christian Medical College at Ludhiana, and the St. Christophers' Training College for women teachers at Madras.

THE STUDENT BODY ON THE CAMPUS OF THE LUCKNOW
CHRISTIAN COLLEGE, INDIA

IN THE BOOKSELLERS' BAZAAR LUCKNOW

IMPORTANCE OF WOMEN'S COLLEGES

There are today seven arts colleges for women in India, four of which are maintained by Christian societies; and three medical colleges for women, two of which are Christian. The importance of these Christian colleges for women is well set forth in the statement of one of their principals, who writes:

"All are agreed that at least some women should receive the highest education that this country can provide. The services of educated women are demanded more and more urgently every year, and they are making themselves felt in every department of the new and varied life of modern India. As wives of educated men, as doctors, teachers, inspectresses, lawyers, secretaries, as workers in every field of philanthropic effort, as persons of great influence in political movements, as leaders in all Christian activities, educated women have already won their footing in India and are becoming a force of great magnitude. We can do no better service to India than to liberate the energies of wisdom and devotion which are latent in her women and to infuse into them the vital ideals of Christianity."[1]

Further tribute to Christian missionaries is given in the following brief quotation:

"A Hindu woman in India, the wife of one of the delegates to the Round Table Conference in London,

---

[1] Dr. Eleanor McDougall, in *Women's Christian College, Madras, 1915-1935*, p. 4.

mentions the fact that her first vision of the ideal of international brotherhood came through a Christian
teacher in an English literature class. Another Hindu
woman, distinguished for her service to India, says that
one of the main sources of her inspiration in public life
has always been the steadfast, fearless willingness to
sacrifice everything to truth, which as a child she had
admired in a missionary teacher."[1]

COEDUCATION

In some parts of India, notably in Madras and Burma
and Assam, where public sentiment was favorable, there
was widespread coeducation at the primary stage even
before the turn of the century. In Christian primary
schools the practice was common everywhere, but there
was no attempt to hurry the pace in higher institutions.
Indian social sentiment, even in the Christian community,
was left to determine policy in this matter. On the other
hand, Christian colleges never debarred girls from their
classes, and even thirty years ago there were occasional
cases of Indian Christian girls studying for their degrees
in men's colleges. Those few courageous girls and their
families were surely pioneers. As time went on their
number grew, especially as women's colleges soon became inadequate to the demand for admission and in

---

[1] Ruth Frances Woodsmall in *Eastern Women Today and Tomorrow*, p.
136. Boston, Central Committee on the United Study of Foreign Missions,
1933.

most cases could not offer facilities for the teaching of science. In some parts of India progressive Hindu sentiment has also been favorable to coeducation, as for example in Poona, where the Fergusson College now possesses a dormitory for eighty girl students who attend college classes with the men.

But for the most part this new development has been seen in the great Christian colleges. At the Scottish Church College in Calcutta and at Forman Christian College, Lahore, there are today half a hundred girl students. In Bombay and Agra there are hostels for women students connected with the mission colleges. At Allahabad Christian College there is a temporary dormitory for girls newly opened in one of the old mission bungalows within the college grounds. Many of the other Christian colleges have increasing numbers of girls who come in as day students from their own homes. This practice is fast gaining ground in the country at large, for the people will not now wait for that indefinitely distant time when the urgent need for women's education might be met by newly established and expensive separate institutions.

PROMINENT WOMEN

No evidence of the necessity and value of Christian education for women can compare with the personalities which it has produced and the work which such women have been able to do in the world. Miss Woodsmall writes, after naming a number of outstanding Indian women:

"With such a body of Christian women leaders in the Orient, together with the great unnamed number of women who in less conspicuous paths of service are radiating Christian influence in the life around them, the Christian movement today may well feel a consciousness of past achievement. . . . . In this effective Christian leadership among Eastern women rests the future promise of the Christian movement in the Orient."[1]

Among many others, the name of Miss Jamila Siraj ud-Din comes to mind. Her father was one of the first Moslem students to give his life to Christ on completing his college education in one of our mission colleges and to enter into the service of the church as a Christian educator. From his Christian home there came sons and daughters to the church, Jamila, the eldest, winning a scholarship for advanced studies abroad in economics. Today she holds the Doctor's degree of Edinburgh University and is the director of women's industries in a great province. On her return to India with her foreign degrees and honors, she was given a great public reception by the prominent men and women of all communities, Christian and non-Christian, who gladly recognized the outstanding Christian influence of her father and mother, and put the stamp of public approval upon her own achievements and public service.

---

[1] Ruth Frances Woodsmall, *Eastern Women Today and Tomorrow*, p. 145 f.

SPECIAL PROBLEMS IN CHRISTIAN HIGHER EDUCATION

We have seen that Christian missions have invariably developed a system of schools and colleges as a necessary part of their Christian task. They have needed them for the development of the Christian family and the life of the church; they have used them as instruments of evangelization, they have employed them in the conviction that the Great Teacher is honored and obeyed in the pursuit and dissemination of knowledge and in the enlightenment which proceeds from the mind to the attitudes and purposes of life; they have been upheld by the belief that the eternal truth of Christ will only be sought and found when men have gained freedom and power to know and shun error and to seek and embrace the truth.[1]

It was inevitable that in an enterprise as extensive as Christian education has become, there should have developed a number of serious problems requiring careful study and united effort at solution. During the past few years various investigations and surveys have been made, the most important and fruitful one being that of the Commission on Christian Higher Education in India, popularly known as the Lindsay Commission, composed of prominent English, American and Indian scholars.

THE LINDSAY COMMISSION

In a statement about the Commission, Dr. Lindsay says:

---

[1] See Table of Educational Statistics p. 217.

"Christianity came to India as a religion of hope and good news. It found itself confronted with views of the world and inherent in the religions of India which taught only resignation and a fatalistic acceptance. The founders of Christian colleges in India rightly thought that the Christian message could only be given in its fullness if it was presented not only as a challenge but as a new view of the world and God. All over the north of India we were told that India, or at least educated India, is rapidly ceasing to be religious. Economic or scientific determinism is becoming the creed of young India. Only Christian knowledge and the Christian view of the world can give hope for despair."

Since the issue of the Lindsay Commission's report, the Christian colleges have given themselves to developing a program of Christian education for the new day. The major recommendations are being continually studied and in great measure applied. They are studying the possibilities of union, specialization, and cooperation; they are examining the possibility of reducing the size and intensifying the Christian quality of college work done with more highly selected students; they are endeavoring to increase the number and proportion of highly trained Indian Christian teachers; they are striving to intensify the personal influence in the colleges upon all who live and study in the circle of a Christian fellowship; they are facing the desire for more Indian responsibility and authority in the management and policy of the colleges; they are examining the need for a closer relationship to Indian culture and national life; they are exploring the avenues of service to the church and nation; they are restudying the essential aims of the colleges in order to make them truly Christian and missionary in these days of intellectual and social and political change; they are laying plans for far greater identification of the Indian church with the support of the colleges, and are issuing a carefully considered appeal for increased participation and help from the Western churches in this day of undreamed-of opportunity.

THE INFLUENCE OF CHRISTIAN INSTITUTIONS

The results of Christian education make an inspiring story. India has today a church of Christ more than six million in number. The leaders of this growing church are products of our Christian schools and colleges. Many of them and many of their fathers received their first knowledge of the gospel in Bible classes in these institutions. Many of them are prominent and influential figures in the councils of the churches and missions and in public affairs. Many of the educated Christian men and women of India have given their lives to the education of their people.

The value to the nation of men who have received Christian training but who may not have become themselves Christian in name, is recognized far and wide and

by non-Christians themselves. Thus Sir Mirza Ismail,
prime minister of Mysore, stated in a public meeting:

"They (missionary schools and colleges) have been a
potent factor in promoting the cause of education and
the spread of enlightenment and culture in the state, as
indeed in India as a whole. One has only to turn to institutions like the Christian College in Madras, the Wilson College in Bombay, the Forman College in Lahore,
to realize the magnitude of the contribution which Christian missions are making to modern India."

No one can fail to see the steady and deep penetration
of Indian life and thought by Christian ideas. This is
recognized by Hindus themselves and frankly confessed.
The late Sir Narayan Chandavarkar, president of the
Bombay Legislative Council and a leading Hindu, said:

"The process of the conversion of India to Christ may
not be going on as rapidly as you hope; nevertheless, I
say, India is being converted. The ideas that lie at the
heart of the gospel are slowly, but surely, permeating
every part of Hindu society and modifying every phase
of Hindu thought."[1]

The Reverend John McKenzie, principal of Wilson
College, Bombay, whose influence on Indian education
may be judged from the fact that for a number of years
he has been vice-chancellor of the Government University of Bombay, writes:

---

[1] Quoted by A. J. Brown, in *One Hundred Years*, p. 663.

"Christian educational institutions have been exercising an enormous influence, intellectually, morally and spiritually, on the lives of those who have studied in them, and through them, on the life of the whole community. It is an influence that has led to comparatively few accessions to the Christian church, but, nevertheless, it is an influence that is Christian, and that is fraught with great significance for the religious life of India and of the world. It is manifest in many ways, but I believe what is most significant is the fact that the eyes of increasing numbers of educated men and women are being turned to Jesus Christ. They are finding in him not merely a great ethical teacher and social reformer, but a great guide in the deep things of the spirit, and a great illuminator of the ways of God in the world."[1]

Hear the testimony of two other men, one an Englishman who has spent a long life in work with college students in India and one an American who addressed great crowds of Indian students at Christian college centers on a recent lecture tour in the East. Canon W. E. S. Holland writes:

"I cannot help but contrast the series of meetings held by E. Stanley Jones with the series I arranged for John R. Mott twenty-five years ago. Dr. Mott spoke to that audience for three nights and dared not mention the name of Jesus Christ until the fourth night, and when

---

[1] From "Higher Education," by John McKenzie, in *The Christian Task in India*, edited by Mr. McKenzie, p. 97. New York, the Macmillan Co., 1929.

he did, the whole meeting broke up in confusion; the leading Hindus stalked out. The name of Jesus Christ stood for everything that they hated. Now, you begin with the name of Christ as your first word; you interpret him for them in the light of their need; they sit here night after night and want more of it. I am astonished at the difference."[1]

Dr. J. Harry Cotton, who gave the lectures in India in 1931-1932 on the Joseph Cook Foundation "for the defense of Christianity in the Orient," reported that "it was a revelation to see the readiness and reverence with which the Oriental students received the lecture on the Cross. At the close of the lecture in Madras, the Hindu chairman, a professor of philosophy in a Hindu university, made this amazing statement to the Hindu audience:

" 'We have been seeking for a fuller revelation of God. We have expected that revelation in terms of overwhelming majesty. We were not prepared for the revelation which came in the face of one who, for the sins of the world, was ready to bear the shame of the Cross.' "[2]

CENTERS OF CHRISTIAN LIFE AND SERVICE

Every Christian school and college constitutes a Christian center of life and fellowship. Nowhere else in the East can you find groups of men and women, Indian,

---

[1] Quoted by A. J. Brown, in *One Hundred Years*, p. 662.
[2] *Ibid.*

European and American, who have so completely learned the happy secret of comradeship in a common life and task. Here are peers and partners enjoying and demonstrating the unity which is found only in Christ. Such a Christian fellowship is a potent factor not only on the campus, and in the homes and lives of the students, but also in the neighborhood and community and city. This feature has not been given sufficient emphasis in the past. Every such institution furnishes a field of Christian effort for its members and stands out as a compact and effective and recognized Christian group in the midst of the non-Christian world.

In such a fellowship scope is also found for common social effort in intimate comradeship with non-Christian students and friends who are actuated by the high Christian motive which they have imbibed. It is in Christian colleges all over India where one finds that organized social service activities have been maintained with high idealism and consistent effort for many years.

Such inspiration for service came to Mohan, who belongs to a very poor but orthodox Hindu family of good caste village cultivators, living in a small mud brick cottage. By cruel self-denial the father sent his boy to the mission high school in hopes that he might qualify himself as a village teacher and thus add to the meagre family income. While in high school, Mohan had the vision of going on to college, in order to be better equipped to give his life to the needs of his village people. He earned his expenses by doing any kind of work, scarcely having enough to eat or to wear. He had been coming for daily morning prayers to the home of one of his professors for over three years. One morning he announced with radiant face, "This is my twentieth birthday. It is also my spiritual birthday, for today I have decided to give my heart to Christ as my Savior." Ever since, he has been making every effort to bring Christ to his village and to win his family. He has organized a social service league of students who are doing rural uplift and educational work in near-by villages. He is also teaching outcaste boys and girls on the college campus to read the Bible. This keen and earnest young man who lives in real poverty said recently, "I am the happiest man in all the world. Jesus has given me everything I need and want. What do you think he would most like to have *me* do for him?" Such students work in partnership with their Christian teachers.

DESIRE FOR CHRISTIAN UNITY

Educated Christian leaders have long been chafing under the disunity of the church. This is discussed in another chapter but we may well mention here the part which Christian schools and colleges have played in bringing about the *will* to union. There are few Christian schools and almost no Christian colleges which have been in a position to recruit their teaching staffs from members of a single Christian denomination. The best available Christian teacher of suitable qualifications is the one who will be appointed. The result has been that almost every Christian institution of higher grade has become the center of an interdenominational Christian community. These families form the backbone of the local church, and furnish increasing numbers of Christian men and women who by conviction and experience stand for a united church. Their voice is being increasingly heard in the ecclesiastical councils where the matter of church union is today assuming major importance.

THE STUDENT CHRISTIAN MOVEMENT

At the present moment plans are being made for the quadrennial conference of the Student Christian Association of India, Burma and Ceylon. For the second time in its history there will gather large numbers of men and women students from the colleges and universities, meeting in combined conference to grapple with the problems which confront the Christian church and Christian youth. Every person who was present at the last quadrennial conference will testify to the feeling of wonder and amazement at the sight of five hundred selected delegates, young men and young women in equal number, representing all the provinces and states as well as the various branches of the Christian church in India, assembled on the beautiful campus of the Allahabad Christian College on the banks of the river Jamna. Never before had such a sight been seen in India. Think what it means to a land where women have lived in seclusion and ignorance, where language and race and religious community separate and divide, that such a company of Christian young people should meet, should share in common meals and games and fellowship, should worship and commune together and should together under able leadership, and in devotion to a common Master, their great Leader, Jesus Christ, face the needs of their beloved country and the opportunity and challenge of Christian service!

The spirit of this unique and epoch-making conference was typified by an answer made by one of the young Christian delegates, to a great Hindu national political leader who came to the conference one day as a guest speaker. In thanking the distinguished Nationalist for his message, in which he had referred to his passion for India's freedom and his longing for better unity between the different races and communities, this courageous young Christian said,—"But the realization of our cherished dreams can be possible only through Jesus Christ, and his spirit and his principles. When he comes to India in all his power, a new heaven and a new earth will dawn for us all."

The Student Christian Association, with its excellent organization and far-reaching influence, is perhaps the most important of the student movements of India today in its effect upon the great work of the Christian church.

WHY MAINTAIN CHRISTIAN COLLEGES IN INDIA?

We may conclude this chapter by asking three questions.

1. Why should an Indian parent or student choose a Christian institution rather than one conducted by the Government or by a private Hindu or Mohammedan society?

The fact is that they do, and in far larger numbers than Christian schools and colleges can admit them. There is something in the study of the Bible and Christian truth, in the presentation of the Christian way of life, in the relationship between the Christian teachers and their pupils, in the character and attitudes and purposes produced by Christian training which proves its own value. Thus Mr. William Paton writes:

"The Christian college has stood for an education rooted and grounded in a religious view of the world. However cabined and confined by the circumstances which have been outlined, it has preserved an ideal of the utmost worth, and every college principal knows of the Hindu and Moslem parents who send their boys to him, hoping earnestly that they will not become Christians and prepared to persecute them if they do, but not less earnestly desiring the moral and spiritual atmosphere which they find in the mission college and usually nowhere else."[1]

---

[1] *Educational Yearbook, 1933,* New York, p. 371. New York, Teachers College, Columbia University, 1933.

2. Why should a missionary or Indian Christian desire to spend his life teaching in a Christian school or college in India?

The first answer to this question assumes that such a teacher is one who believes sincerely in the Lord Jesus Christ and desires to proclaim and share his faith. Having faced the fundamental requirements of Christian conviction and purpose, and finding here the opportunity to witness and share, the teacher may go on to discover also the satisfaction of living in a group where Christian unity is found, the stimulus of contact with those who represent the churches of East and West, and the consciousness that the young men and young women under his care are being enriched and inspired by all these relationships as well as by the instruction and discipline which they are receiving.

3. Why should the church be interested in a Christian school or college in India?

We are interested because such colleges represent the only agency maintained to select and train the Christian leaders of the church and of the nation, the men and women who will bring to bear on Indian thought and society and life the great Christian principles of individual character and social justice.

"It is the aim of the Christian college to stem the tide of doubt or atheism by presenting faith in Christ as a true, rational and workable faith, the only faith that will save India and satisfy its age-long yearning after God."[1]

In these momentous days of India's history there is the necessity as never before for the highest type of educated leaders, men and women with Christian ideals and of Christian quality and purpose, if that great people is to go steadily forward on the path of national realization.

A STATESMAN'S ESTIMATE

Indeed the colleges of India may well have a function to perform which is of utmost necessity to the world today. The Marquis of Lothian, who was a member of the Parliamentary Select Committee entrusted with the task of preparing the draft of the reformed Constitution for India, has called attention to the extraordinary significance of the Christian colleges of India for the world. Speaking in New York in 1934 on the approaching change in the form of India's government, and the existing communal and religious divisions in India, he said:

"In this situation is there any force comparable to that which can be exercised by the Indian Christian colleges for bridging these interior gulfs and for producing the kind of leader who can lead India toward both unity and freedom in the terrific experiment which is being launched today? The spirit of Christ shining through those institutions can transform much of young India,

---

[1] F. M. Velte, "Christian Colleges and the Students of India," in *The Presbyterian*, January, 1937.

and so produce leaders who are immune to or who can surmount the communal feeling.

"The work that can be done by the Indian Christian colleges is not only of value to India but of supreme value to the world. If the Indian experiment fails, if co-operation between Great Britain and India during the next ten or fifteen difficult years breaks down, whether through the inability of the British to move fast enough, to put themselves into the shoes of another nation, or whether through the inability of India to settle down to the practical working of the Constitution, the result will be further chaos for the world. So I feel very deeply that the Indian Christian colleges have an immensely important work to do, a work not only for India, as important as it is, but even more for the whole of humanity in the present day."

CHAPTER VI

THE CHRISTIAN CHURCH IN INDIA

By THE RT. REV. V. S. AZARIAH, Bishop of Dornakal

W E are attending church on a Sunday morning in a city of South India. This particular church belongs to the Anglican Communion, but much that we see will be found also among the non-Roman churches everywhere, although these are divided into about a hundred and fifty different groups.

The church has pews as in American churches. Long before the service begins the church is full; in fact people hasten to church as soon as the first bell rings half an hour before service time, for fear of failing to get a seat. A few of the men and young men are clad in European costume, whereas the women without exception are dressed in the beautiful silk *saris* of various colors, which are universally recognized as the dress of Indian ladies. The men sit on one side and the women on the other. Every man and woman carries the Book of Common Prayer, a Directory of Worship, a hymn book, and a big vernacular Bible. The women's heads are covered with their *saris*.

When the second bell stops every seat is taken. A processional voluntary is played on an organ or harmonium.

Worship according to the exact pattern of the particular church's ecclesiastical mother is followed. The hymns sung are translations of the English or German originals, set to the original tune. Very probably also one or two lyrics sung are set to Indian airs. The offerings are usually generous. The orderliness, the reverence and the outward respectability of the congregation strikes us as of a very high order. We walk in and join the worship, and thank God for the high standard achieved by the educated Christian community.

There are, however, certain things that may sadden us: the totally foreign character of the service, the foreign hymnology and melodies, the Western organ or harmonium played even in accompaniment to the indigenous tunes, the foreign architecture of the sacred edifice, the pews, so incongruous in a place of worship in India and so inconveniently arranged that they make kneeling for prayer difficult, if not impossible. These are all blemishes that will only be detected by trained eyes; they are the heritage of the past, copies of Western church architecture innocently introduced by the early missionaries. The growth of Nationalism; the new ideas that are taking hold of the younger missionaries as well as Indian Christians of the present generation; the experiments going on here and there of adapting indigenous temple architecture to Christian church buildings; encouragement given to Indian music, and to other external accompaniments of worship—these all point toward a better future.

A Village Church

Several miles from the city we visit another church; a rural church in a Telugu village. Our car cannot comfortably enter the village, but a band of village young men meets us outside to push it along the sandy path. This path has been prepared especially for the visitors— a mound here has been knocked down, a pit there filled up, and a branch above lopped off. We pass right through the aristocratic quarters of the village, for the dwellings of the caste people have to be passed before one comes to the outcaste quarters where the church is situated. Flags and bunting are profusely in evidence, and in arches, probably a little triangular and bent in parts, are signs made of colored paper with "Welcome" (sometimes spelt with a double "l!") in English. Rows of men, women and children greet us outside the church and we go in with them.

All the people are cleanly dressed, the men with shirts, a few perhaps with coats, on one side, and the women in beautiful white and colored *saris* on the other, all seated on the floor, which is covered with palm leaf mats. A lyric is started and lustily sung, to the accompaniment of a drum, perhaps a violin or two, and certainly a pair of cymbals to beat time. The beauty of Indian music does not consist in the blending of various parts into rich harmony, but in the rhythmic swing of its cadence enriched by drum and cymbals. With such indigenous accompaniments Christian hymns are sung to

native tunes, which sweetly speak to the Indian heart.
The people, very obviously, enter into the singing with
their whole heart and soul and we, the spectators, even
though we may not understand, cannot fail to be stirred
by the swing of the melody and almost unconsciously
led to adoration and worship.

With this preparation, the service begins. If we are in
an Anglican church the *Venite* (Psalm 95) is sung to an
Indian tune, the psalms are sung not to a foreign chant,
but to a Telugu lyric, the *Te Deum* is most attractively
rendered in the same way, the Creed is recited, and brief
prayers are said. Instruction is then given through the
catechetical method: the people answer questions or
complete a quotation from Scripture.

Finally come the offerings. The congregation remains
seated, singing. Women walk up to the minister and
hand him little bags or empty them in their proper
places. These contain the handfuls of grain or flour set
apart as God's portion each time a meal was cooked during the previous week. Some women may have also in
their hands a few beans, a pumpkin, snake-gourds, or
cucumbers raised in their private gardens if these are in
season. Perhaps there are also one or two eggs. The
offerings made, the whole congregation stands up in
silence, the singing is stopped, the minister walks down
the aisle with the alms basin and empties into it the
contents of the brass vessels that stand on the pedestals
in the body of the church, and says a prayer, lifting up

to God the offerings of the people, who say "Amen," still all standing. No collection plates are passed around; every worshipper on entering the church deposits his offering of coins in these vessels. Perhaps a prayer is said and the minister retires; the congregation sing a recessional lyric, kneel reverently, and depart after a short private prayer.

Such a service may be seen any Sunday of the year in any Anglican church in the Dornakal diocese; but apart from the use of the forms prescribed in the Book of Common Prayer, the same type of worship may be seen in any one of the non-Episcopal churches. The sitting on the floor, the Indian music, the indigenous lyrics, the cleanliness and reverence of the worshippers; the offerings in kind and in coin, are common to all.

Every area in India contains in it a few town churches of the first type and a large number of rural churches of the second type. Four-fifths of all India's people dwell in villages having five hundred persons and under, and only eleven per cent live in towns of five thousand and more. Hence if India is to be evangelized, the villages must be evangelized; if an indigenous church is to be built up, it should be the rural church.

STAGES OF MISSIONARY WORK

The first stage of missionary work opens when the missionary begins the task of evangelization, and either alone or with a few Indian assistants from a neighboring older field goes about itinerating in his area, proclaiming the message of salvation. When the first converts are made, they are baptized and the nucleus of a church comes into being. The missionary naturally becomes the leader, the shepherd and the pastor of his converts. This perhaps goes on for a number of years. During all this time the missionary is all-important.

The second stage may be said to begin when the missionary has succeeded in bringing some of the converts to communicant status. A son of early converts is made a minister of the church. The task of the missionary from that moment on will be to associate this indigenous minister and the church with himself; to take the pastor into his fullest confidence; to place upon members of the church the responsibility for the evangelization of their countrymen; to impart to them the missionary zeal that inspired him to come out of his native land to be a messenger of Christ to a foreign people. In this second stage the missionary is not all-important; he is the leader, and the Indian minister is his helper.

But soon must come the third stage, when in this indigenous church with an indigenous ministry there is an organization under councils or synods. At this stage the church must become the primary factor, the missionary its helper. He may be the chairman of the church council, or one of his former assistants may be the chairman. Whatever his official position may be, he will recognize that he is not the "boss." The Christian task is not his, but the church's. The work must henceforth be, not mission-centric, but church-centric. His Christian heritage, his spiritual experience, his superior learning will still give him a position of moral and spiritual leadership. He still will be needed to inspire and guide the infant church. His services still will be required to impart to the young in school and college the hope of the future, to train teachers and ministers, the future leaders and guides of the church, and to be the medium of communication between his home church and this daughter church, and thus the mediator between this church and the holy catholic church of Western Christendom.

This is the third stage, when the church is given recognition as the important factor in the Christianization of the land. The missionary will constantly keep before his mind that this church is the local representative of the body of Christ, in which his spirit dwells; that it is that church's privilege and function to witness to the world of its Savior and Lord; that it is its birthright to develop and grow in accordance with the life of God implanted in it; and that it must exhibit that life in characteristics true to the soil in which it is planted. Ever will be on his lips the words of John the Baptist adapted to the case: It (the church) must increase and I (the missionary) must decrease. Most mission fields have great need of such large-hearted missionaries.

THE INDIAN CHURCH DEFINED

One of the most important results achieved by the World Missionary Conference at Edinburgh in 1910 was the recognition it gave to the church in the mission field. The chairman of the commission on the church in the mission field used these memorable words, which might be said to sum up the finding of the commission: "You have now what we begin to call not a little but a great church, ... established in the very heart of the pagan world, ... the young Christian church which missions have founded, but which is itself now the great mission to the non-Christian world."[1] The indigenous church has since then been unquestionably acknowledged to be the greatest, the most potent and the most natural factor in the evangelization of any country. On the efficiency, the purity and witness of this church the Christianization of that country will ultimately depend.

But, alas, what we call the Indian church is not one entity. The divisions of Christendom make it impossible for twentieth century Christians of any country to belong to a single ecclesiastical organization. There are in consequence as many churches and groups in India as there are those who send out missionaries from the West. Further, it must be said that in this chapter we are leaving out of consideration the 300,000 who belong to the various European races and to the Anglo-Indian

---

[1] From *The Church in the Mission Field;* Report of Commission II, p. 341.

community, though these latter are truly indigenous. In the early years of missionary enterprise the Anglo-Indian community were often very closely associated with missionaries from abroad in the work of evangelization, education, and in the production of Christian literature. They are still capable of playing a great part in missionary work.

In this chapter, the Indian church will mean the Indian members of the churches, leaving out of account those who have their services conducted for them in the English language and who truly may be called the English church in India. The Indian church in this chapter is the theoretical aggregate of the indigenous Christians in all the churches, owning very many different church loyalties, following many forms of differing ecclesiastical traditions, worshipping in many Indian languages, with a great variety of form and ritual throughout the length and breadth of this vast continent. There are a few affirmations that may be made of them all: they are all classified as Indian Christians for government purposes, they worship in one of the two hundred languages and dialects of India, they have a distinct religious genius, which finds expression in their formularies of worship and in the directing of their common life, even though they remain members of different Christian bodies. On them both separately and together lies the responsibility for making our Lord known to their countrymen.

The total Indian Christian community in India and Burma in the year 1931 was 5,990,234, of whom two-thirds are in South India, that is in the Madras Presidency and the states of Hyderabad, Mysore, and Travancore adjoining it. About two and a half millions are Roman Catholics and Romo-Syrians, half a million are Syrian Christians, the remaining three millions are connected with non-Roman and non-Syrian churches. India has then the largest indigenous Christian community in all Asia.

The rate of increase of the Indian Christian population from 1872-1931 was as follows:

1872-1881	22	per cent
1881-1891	34	per cent
1891-1901	31	per cent
1901-1911	34	per cent
1911-1921	25	per cent
1921-1931	34	per cent

During the decade 1921-1931

Buddhists increased	10.5	per cent
Moslems increased	13	per cent
Hindus increased	10.4	per cent
Christians increased (non-Roman)	41	per cent

The oldest Christian community in India is that of the Syrian Christians, in the state of Travancore. Tradition connects the introduction of Christianity into Travancore with the apostle St. Thomas. Most scholars are agreed that there is no historical proof to discredit this tradition.

There were in the year 1931 a total of 1,180,546 Syrian Christians, a fifth of the entire Christian population of India. This number is unfortunately distributed among many churches of different loyalties: the Orthodox Jacobite, the Reformed, the Chaldean, the Roman and the Anglican. All the sections of the Syrian churches are presided over by Indian bishops and have always been independent of foreign support. Perhaps the most alive and growing section of all is the Reformed Church of St. Thomas. Besides supporting a large number of priests and evangelists in Travancore, this church has undertaken missionary work of its own in Cochin and North Kanara. In general education, in high ideals of Christian conduct, and in capacity for leadership the Syrian Christians are second to none in India.

The majority of the rest of the Christian community belongs to the Roman communion. They number 2,113,-000. They are found in all parts of the country, and in large numbers in the provinces of Madras, Bombay, Bengal, Bihar and Orissa. The greatest and one of the earliest missionaries of the Roman church was Francis Xavier, who landed in India in 1543 and founded the church in the coastal villages and towns in South India. The Roman Catholic Church has done a great work in the educational field. Loyala College in

Madras and St. Joseph's College in Trichinopoly are instances. By their exclusive claims and indiscriminate invasion of the territories of other missions and churches, they often interfere with the discipline of these other churches and make it very difficult for others to entertain feelings of Christian friendliness with them.

ORGANIZATION

The administrative organization of the Indian churches naturally varies according to the ecclesiastical tradition of the particular church that founded them. The Indian churches under the nurture of the Lutherans naturally follow the Lutheran church model in government, worship, and teaching; those under the Methodists similarly follow the Methodist pattern; those under Anglican or Independent churches likewise are organized on those patterns. But probably some such general form as follows may be true under all ecclesiastical polities.

We begin from a village unit. A village or a group of two or three villages are placed under the care of a teacher and his wife. Fifteen or twenty-five such groups with about ten to fifteen teachers are shepherded by an ordained minister or pastor. A pastorate committee (or the quarterly meeting or church committee) consisting of the pastor or chairman and a number of lay members elected by the communicants, assist the pastor in the general administration. In all church organizations Indian laymen predominate. The pastorate committee usually has charge of the local church expenses, administration of the poor fund, and the people's offerings for the support of their ministry and the supervision of all church property in the locality. They also assist the pastor in the maintaining of church discipline and in the oversight of the parish schools.

As a rule these Indian church committees have to do only with the funds they themselves raise and are responsible only for the departments of church work carried on with these limited resources. It is, however, becoming increasingly the practice in most missions to place greater responsibilities on the district councils and to make them grants from the missionary society, enabling them to carry on their budget all elementary education, local evangelization, and all pastoral work wherever such responsibilities are placed upon the Indian church. Where leadership is in the hands of capable and spiritually minded Indian ministers it has been invariably found to result in increased offerings from the people for the work of the church; and in greater realization of their responsibility for the support of their ministry and for the evangelization of their country. The acceptance of such responsibilities brings with it greater dependence upon divine resources and therefore a richer spiritual experience to leaders and the people.

As soon as there is a communicant membership in a

village or in a group of villages, they should be organized under a pastorate committee so that from the very beginning the responsibility for evangelism, for discipline, and for the administration of funds may be shared by the chosen representatives of the people. Where this is delayed, the congregations tend to lean upon the missionary, a dependence which is wholly inimical to true development. It is also important that from the very outset young people should be picked for higher training in residential schools and given opportunities of self-development in order that from among them an indigenous ministry may be raised up. Such residential schools are a feature in all missions. The children can as a rule be supported by scholarships of twenty-five dollars a year. An indigenous ministry promotes Christian giving and hastens local ministerial support. Lack of such giving, however, should not be made an argument for keeping congregations under foreign pastoral supervision.

ECCLESIASTICAL ORGANIZATIONS

A feature of Indian church life in the twentieth century is the setting up of ecclesiastical organizations in different parts of India.

In the year 1907 the Presbyterian and Congregational churches of South India formed themselves into the South India United Church. The churches established through the missionary agencies of the American Board of Commissioners for Foreign Missions, the Reformed Church in America, the Church of Scotland, and the United Free Church of Scotland form the constituent parts of this church. Its supreme governing body is the General Assembly, which meets once every two years and more than once Indians have been elected to the moderatorship. Its total Christian community in 1936 was about 263,000, of whom 53,000 were communicants, ministered to by about 240 ordained ministers.

The United Church of Northern India is a similar ecclesiastical organization formed in 1924 through the union of the Presbyterian Church in India and the Congregational Churches of Western India. At the time of union the former group, which had been organized in 1905, combined various churches of Presbyterian polity in North India, established by the missions of the American, Scotch, Irish, Welsh, Australian, New Zealand and Canadian Presbyterian churches. At the end of 1935, there was affiliated with the church a total baptized community of 251,706 of whom 77,350 were communicant members. In 1931 the ordained ministers of the United Church numbered 444.

The Federation of Evangelical Lutheran Churches is an organization established in 1926. The churches of American and of Continental Lutheran origin having mother boards in the United States, Denmark, Sweden, Germany, Switzerland, are in this federation.

The Church of England in India had always been by

statute subject to the Archbishop of Canterbury and the British Parliament. The bishoprics of Calcutta, Madras and Bombay were created by act of Parliament. For the creation of every subsequent diocese parliamentary sanction had to be sought, and no consecration of a bishop could be undertaken without a mandate from the King. The legal connection between the Church of England in India and the Church of England in Britain was, at the request of the former, severed in 1927 by the passing of the Indian Church Measure by the National Assembly of the Church of England. From March 1, 1930, the Anglican church in India took the name "Church of India, Burma and Ceylon" and became an autonomous branch of the Anglican communion. Its total membership in the year 1934 was 450,000, shepherded by 1,179 ordained ministers, of whom 212 were ministering to English congregations. These creations have been instrumental in bringing to the people a church consciousness which has been most valuable.

INDIAN LEADERSHIP

The National Missionary Council (now the National Christian Council of India, Burma, and Ceylon), at its very first session in 1912, emphasized the necessity for the development of Indian leadership. One of its resolutions recorded the conviction "that whenever capable and spiritually minded men and women are discovered, churches and missions should make a real and unmis-

takable advance by placing Indians on a footing of complete equality, in status and responsibility, with Europeans and thus open for them the highest and the
most responsible positions in every department of missionary activity." In this connection the Council also
emphasized the principle that the work carried on by
foreign missionary societies should be gradually transferred, as opportunities offered, to the Indian church,
and that suitable modifications of existing organizations
should be adopted, wherever necessary, so that this
principle might be carried out by missionary bodies.

The past twenty-five years have seen an enormous
development in the direction contemplated in that reso-
lution. In many areas, charges of districts once held by
missionaries from abroad have now been transferred to
suitable Indian leaders. Educational institutions and
hospitals once under foreign control have been placed
under Indian supervision. In some areas "the superin-
tending missionary" no longer exists; his huge districts
have been sub-divided and placed under Indian ministers. In handling mission funds and accounts, in keeping the work at an efficient standard, and in the vigilant
and firm exercise of discipline over their subordinate
fellow workers, many Indian Christians are proving
themselves worthy of the trust placed in their hands.
Such leaders, however, are not plentiful. On the one
hand, far more Indian leaders of this type are needed
than are available at present; and on the other hand, a

still bolder policy is essential in all missions and churches of entrusting to Indians greater and greater responsibilities. The carrying of responsibility trains character, develops leadership, and drives men to throw themselves upon God. At a time when the spirit of Nationalism sweeps over the land, and all that is un-Indian is looked upon with suspicion, it is vital that everything possible should be done both in appearance and in reality to identify the Christian movement with the indigenous church and indigenous leadership.

THE CHURCH IN INDIAN CIVIC LIFE

The Indian Christian's increasing freedom from caste prejudice and partisanship, his general uprightness in conduct, his early training in residential schools and colleges under men and women educators of supreme sacrifice and devotion, ought to fit him to be preeminently an officer of high efficiency in the state service. That this is so is shown by the recognition given to Indian Christians by people and Government. In speaking to an Indian Christian audience in South India, the European district officer said that "the church has contributed an ever increasing number of able officers to the public services and also given a large percentage of good and able men to other professions." At the time of writing this, three states have Indian Christian prime ministers; some of the largest municipal corporations have or have had Indian Christian executive officers or commissioners often selected by non-Christian councilors. Hindu princes and rulers have invited qualified Indian Christians to become headmasters for their Hindu high schools. The fact that these and similar appointments are acceptably held by members of the community indicates that the service that the Christian Indian can render to national life is unlimited.

Indian Christians, though numerically small, are well in advance of others in education and literacy. Of the 6,000,000 Indian Christians, 1,148,325, or 21 per cent, are literate. This percentage is higher than that of Hindus, Moslems, or Sikhs. The Indian Christian women stand well ahead of all in the matter of education, the proportion per thousand being 15 for Moslems, 21 for Hindus, and 148 for Indian Christians. Only the Parsees, a small highly cultured group, exceed this proportion.

The proportion of literacy among Christians is by no means sufficient, of course. Every effort is being made to raise it, for the church cannot rest satisfied until every boy and girl, man and woman can read the Bible. The problem while urgent cannot be solved immediately or without much patient and continuous work. It is, however, gratifying to note that despite large numbers of illiterate people coming into the church year after year, literacy among Christians in India fell only 1.5 per thousand between 1921 and 1931.

While we thus frankly face the problem of literacy of the Indian Christian community we cannot shut our eyes to the great advance already made. Whereas Christians constitute only about one and a half per cent of the population, seven per cent of those engaged in the teaching profession are Christians. There is probably no other community that has such a large proportion of its total number engaged in imparting primary education. To become the teachers of young India and to spread through the length and breadth of that land the blessings of education is no mean privilege. The service rendered through this one channel alone ought to justify the claim of the Indian church to be one of the most powerful factors in the regeneration of the land.

CHRISTIAN GIVING

Thus far nothing has been said about self-support—that ubiquitous word found in all modern missionary literature. I am second to none in my desire to see Indian Christians realize their stewardship of all they possess and the duty of Christian giving. Christian life cannot be healthy and complete unless it exhibits this grace also. Those who dedicate themselves to the Lord will certainly dedicate their money also. Those who profess to love the Lord must love him with all their soul, with all their mind and with all their strength. So much money means just so much intellectual ability or physical power or happy inheritance, and these should surely be dedicated to God, if one professes to be his.

Notwithstanding all this conviction I am conscious

that very often insistence on self-support as the first duty of a church, or as the index of a church's capacity to accept responsibilities, or as the preliminary requisite of self-government or freedom, can do as great harm to the spiritual life of the indigenous church as to that of the older church. Spiritual values cannot be measured by material standards. To say that a church's first business is to pay the salaries of its ministers and that a congregation can only administer funds that they themselves give, is to apply to the Indian church principles which do not apply to many state-aided churches of Europe, nor to churches partly supported by home mission funds in the United States. Let the placing of responsibility upon the churches and the participation of the leaders in all the councils of the churches go on as fast as these churches show fitness and desire for such responsibilities. Let the missionary and mission boards definitely train the church for these responsibilities, and let Christian giving be cultivated in the church as all other virtues are, through teaching, prayer and example.

We lack sufficient information from all missions and churches to enable us to state accurately how much Indian Christians contribute of their substance to the support of Christian work. In many fields vast sums of money are collected for the construction of churches and chapels and their repairs that do not come into mission purview. Further, what the people contribute in personal labor for the construction of churches, schools

and teachers' and ministers' houses is most difficult of
appraisal in rupees, annas and pies. There is also this
further difficulty: the proportion of giving per baptized
Christian differs in different areas according to the earning capacity of the people. In South India the average
for a whole district was a dollar a year for every communicant member. In the backward communities in the
Telugu country it is generally about eighty cents a year
for each communicant. Comparing the earning power
of the Indian unskilled laborer with that of the West-
erner, this is a very good proportion.

The contributions of the people are also increased by
the adoption of methods that will appeal to them. They
enjoy harvest festivals and they love to bring to God
a portion of their harvest produce. Rice or flour collection is another popular way of enabling them to
make a regular offering. First fruits, first egg, first-born
of cattle, first month's salary or first days' wages—all
these have a fascination for the Indian mind. The poor
Indian Christian has scarcely ever any ready cash at his
disposal. His wages are often in kind; his offerings must
be in kind too. Calves, lambs, sheep, cattle, hundreds
of chickens, sacks of rice or other grain may all be seen
among the thank offerings brought to the church on
such festival occasions. It often is said by Indian Christians that offerings must be requested for God, and not
to pay the salary of the teacher or pastor. Neither in the
Hindu or the Moslem system do priests receive a fixed

salary from the people to whom they minister. Offerings are made to the deity in the temple; they may be utilized for any good purpose. For this reason in some churches the offerings are not collected, but are offered. Collections must go; offerings will remain.

MOVEMENTS TOWARDS UNITY

The divisions of Christendom are a source of weakness and inefficiency in the West; they are a crime and scandal in the non-Christian world. Union is a desirable ideal in the older churches; it is a matter of life and death in the younger churches in Africa and the East. It has been said that the resources in men and money at the disposal of the existing missionary agencies are abundantly adequate to evangelize the world. Yet they are actually woefully insufficient because of the wastage due to overlappings, competition and rivalries inevitable in a divided Christendom. Moreover, the non-Christian is bewildered by Christian separations. Compared with these, the sects within Hinduism, Islam, and Sikhism appear to him as nothing. A leader of the depressed classes, speaking of the movement among his people away from Hinduism, said: "When Christianity is suggested as a possible religion they point out that they are united in Hinduism, but will be divided in Christianity; and I have no answer to give!" Have Christians any answer to give?

Indian Christians are one in their allegiance to the

Savior, one in national and political aspirations, one in
their responsibility for bringing their countrymen to
Christ. They are not one in their witness to truth, not
one in public worship, not one in baptism, not one in
ministry, and therefore not one in participation of the
holy communion—the sacrament of unity. Moreover,
there is the pathetic fact that they are not responsible
for these divisions. They are in different ecclesiastical
groups not because of theology but because of geog-
raphy. An Indian Christian is what he is because a particular Western church happened to evangelize that
particular tract of country where he or his parents happened to live, and so he was baptized into the fellowship of that particular church. Later of course he was
inoculated with the virus of denominationalism and was
taught to believe that his was the only true form of the
holy catholic church and that all other churches were
in error! On the whole, however, these divisions do not
appeal to the Indian Christians. Faced with the titanic
task of the winning of India for Christ—in the words
of the Tranquebar manifesto—they find themselves
rendered weak and relatively impotent by these unhappy
divisions, divisions for which they were not responsible
and which were imposed upon them from without,
divisions which they did not create and which they do
not desire to perpetuate.

This is a problem that the Indian churches cannot
solve without the cooperation of the mother churches.

These younger churches are dependent to such a large degree upon the older churches for leadership, guidance and financial assistance that they simply cannot act without the good will and cooperation of the latter. The sin, therefore, of perpetuating a divided state of Christendom throughout the mission field lies certainly upon the heads of the older churches.

Attempts have been made from time to time to heal these divisions both in the East and West. We have only to recall as instances the inauguration of the United Church of Canada, the Methodist Church of Great Britain, and the Church of Scotland, and the establishment of intercommunion between the National Church of Sweden and the Anglican communion. These unions have had their wholesome repercussions in the mission field.

The South India United Church, already referred to, is one such accomplished union. A still bolder attempt is being made in South India to bring together into one united church this South India United Church, the (Wesleyan) Methodist church, and the Anglican church in India. A manifesto was issued by Indian ministers from Tranquebar in March, 1919. Representatives officially appointed by the three churches have worked together for the past eighteen years and have formulated a scheme of union,[1] which is being examined and considered by

---

[1] *Proposed Scheme of Union,* published by Christian Literature Society, Madras, India.

the churches concerned. This is the first instance of a serious attempt to bring into one organic union churches following Episcopal and non-Episcopal traditions. If consummated, it will afford a model for negotiations for similar union all over the world. Its importance therefore cannot be overestimated.

FELLOWSHIP AND COOPERATION

While union of the churches is the ideal, and ought to be the goal of our efforts and prayers, much can be done meanwhile to minimize the evils of division, through the fellowship and cooperation made possible by the National Christian Council, and its auxiliaries the Provincial Councils, established in the provinces. This Council is the result of the statesmanship and organizing ability of Dr. John R. Mott, to whom modern missions owe the initiation of the International Missionary Council and the national councils of various lands, which were an outcome of the first World Missionary Conference held at Edinburgh in 1910. The objects of the National Christian Council are "to stimulate thinking and investigation on missionary questions; to enlist in the solution of these questions the best knowledge and experience to be found in India and to make the results available for all churches and missions in India; to help to coordinate the activities of the Provincial Councils; and through common consultation to help to form Christian public opinion and bring it to bear on the moral and social problems of the day." It is acknowledged by all that these functions are being efficiently performed by the Council to the great gain of the Christian enterprise throughout India. The Fraser Commission on Village Education, the Mass Movement Survey under the leadership of Bishop Pickett, the Lindsay Commission on Christian Colleges, the Five-Year Forward Movement in Evangelism, the Mission of Fellowship to Great Britain—these are some of the outstanding tasks initiated and carried out under its auspices.

SPIRITUAL LIFE AND WITNESS-BEARING

Another ever present problem is the maintenance and deepening of the spiritual life of the Christians. The problem becomes vital in areas where the Christian community is of the second and succeeding generations. The converts of the first generation usually exhibit all the glow and warmth of their new experience. The sacrifices they made for the sake of Christ brought with them a rich reward of fellowship with God and joy in his service. The children of the second and third generation, however, while heirs to Christian nurture and upbringing, cannot be said to inherit Christian experience.

The Indian religious instinct is a great asset to the Christians and they are all generally known to be religious as far as outward conformity goes. Their attendance at public worship, their observance of the sacraments, and their adherence to the Christian pattern of life are most praiseworthy. But to bring Christian life to its full fruitage there is required careful training and cultivation in such matters as personal faith in the living God through Jesus Christ, trust and reliance upon him through all the changing vicissitudes of life, fellowship of the Holy Spirit maintained by study of Holy Scripture and private prayer, and exhibition of the Christ-life in business, in the home, in all social relationships, in marriage affiliations, in public and civic life. How can this be done? How far has this task been attempted or accomplished?

These are not the exclusive problems of the mission field; equally do they affect the churches in the West. They will not solve themselves while we ignore them; they require vigilant study and careful planning by a sanctified ministry. For a church surrounded by the deadening atmosphere of non-Christian faiths, the question of keeping up the Christian ideals of faith and conduct are vital.

In securing this result a Christian home is an indispensable prerequisite. A home where the highest standards of Christian conduct are expected from every member of the family, where family worship is the natural climax of an all-day Christian life, where the Lord's day is honored and sanctified for renewal of body and spirit, where the child learns the elementary facts of the Christian religion from his mother's lips—such a home cannot but transmit religion from one generation to another.

Organizations like the Mothers' Union are invaluable in keeping these ideals ever before Christian mothers.

Religious education is another factor. It is the opinion of the writer that in the field of Christian education there is opportunity for a large number of consecrated men and women missionaries to mold the lives of the younger generation and inspire them to the service of their church and people.

A third factor is adult education. It is not sufficient to aim at the education of the young, for a large percentage of adult Christians are illiterate. With growth in literacy of children and adults will come the demand for new books, and if the Christian agencies do not provide these, the literacy attained will pass away, to the great loss of the individual and the church.

A fourth factor in keeping alive the flame of religion in the second and later generations of Christians is keeping the duty of witness-bearing constantly before them. Christian life will never thrive where witness-bearing and service for others are neglected. Whatever Christianity is, it is not a selfish religion. It was founded by one who saved others, and himself he could not save. There is no Christian life which does not include in it the element of saving others. The temptation to seek one's own salvation and to neglect that of others is particularly subtle to the Indian. His ancestral religion taught him to concentrate all his energies on attaining *mukti,* or freedom. If from the very outset Christians could be taught the duty of saving others as an inseparable part of the Christian duty, they would escape the stagnation and deadness that is often complained of in the second and later generation Christians.

Churches are alive to this situation. The National Christian Council has taken certain steps to insure that the call to evangelism will be given to every Christian. The Forward Movement in Evangelism launched in the year 1935 has placed before all the churches a definite five-year plan. A Week of Witness is also being widely observed. In one church in the Telugu area 28,000 Christians took part in giving their testimony to their non-Christian neighbors, selling over 30,000 gospel portions. The result of this mass witnessing was that 8,000 were reported as desiring to be instructed for baptism! But very often this cannot be done until the support of teachers to give instruction can be found; this averages seventy-five dollars a year.

MISSIONARY WORK OF THE INDIAN CHURCH

Mention must also be made of the organized missionary effort of the Indian church in different parts of the country. Several churches in South India have small home missionary societies of their own, which employ evangelists in their own or neighboring areas. The churches in the American Madura Mission area, and of the Jaffna area, and the Telugu Baptist Convention are supporting such activities.

THE RIGHT REVEREND V. S. AZARIAH, D.D.
BISHOP OF DORNAKAL

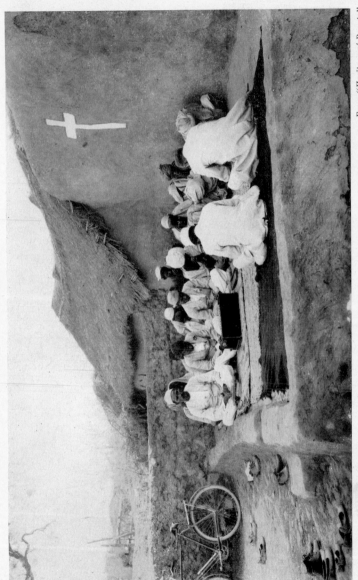

The Indian Missionary Society of Tinnevelly, organized in 1903 by the Anglican church in the Diocese of Tinnevelly, now supports three Indian missionaries in Dornakal at a distance of over eight hundred miles from the home base. Besides supporting the three Tamil men, it is carrying on its budget a staff of fifty-six Telugu teachers, two Telugu clergymen, and has gathered a Christian community of over twelve thousand persons. The income of the society in the year 1936 was $8,500.

The National Missionary Society of India was organized in 1906 by representatives of Indian churches from all parts of India. It aims at uniting all Christian communions in all the provinces into one organization for the evangelization of India—though the fields for work are assigned to churches fully respecting ecclesiastical allegiances. The society, like the one in Tinnevelly, stands for the three fold principle: Indian men, Indian money, and Indian management. This society carries on work in nine provinces. The total income of the society in 1934 was $31,200, which supports 160 workers shepherding altogether about 10,000 converts.

The total gain to the Christian enterprise in India through all these and other indigenous agencies may not appear to be very large in volume. They are, however, so many evidences that the Indian churches are realizing their responsibility for the evangelization of their country and are contributing their little share to the Christian movement, not only by preaching and teaching but largely by example. I have in my diocese 210,000 Christians, the great majority of these being drawn from outcastes. But there are about 35,000 converts from the high castes and middle-class communities, and these have all come in during the last six or seven years. When you ask the reason why they have become Christians they say: "We have seen the change that has come over the lives of the outcastes and we want to have this religion too."

We have endeavored in this chapter to present a picture of the Indian church as it is today in its most hopeful features and activities. On the purity, sacrifice and devotion of this church depends ultimately the Christianization of India. To equip it for this task, to educate and train its youth, to inspire it to fulfill its high calling is a service that the churches in America can render at this time.

The church in India beckons to its partners in Europe and America and cries:

Come over and help us. Help us to meet the opportunity that is open to us at the present time to present the gospel to the three hundred and fifty-two millions of our countrymen. Help us to instruct, baptize and organize those who are coming everywhere into the life of fellowship of the Christian church.

Help us to teach the young, to remove adult illiteracy, and to provide vernacular literature for those who are emerging from darkness into light.

Help us to train teachers, to provide an Indian ministry and to inspire our churches for their evangelistic task.

Help us to come into closer fellowship and unity that we may all be one—that the world may believe in the divine mission of Jesus Christ.

Help us by your prayers that India may become Christ's and may bring her glory and riches into the City of God.

Then shall be fulfilled the vision of the seer: The kingdoms of this world are become the kingdoms of our Lord and of his Christ; and HE SHALL REIGN FOREVER AND EVER.

CHAPTER VII

FACING THE FUTURE TASK

By E. Stanley Jones

I. The Christian Approach to India

THE Christian approach to India was never more promising and never more perplexing; we have never had more opportunity and never more opposition.

With the break-up of the older forms of faith, with the inward decay of ancient beliefs, with perplexity and spiritual hunger that comes from spiritual insecurity and uncertainty, with the strain that has come through the going to pieces of the social order upon which men have leaned, with the outcastes declaring they are leaving their old customs and faith, the opportunity for Christian missions was never so great as in India at the present time. The whole situation cries to high heaven for some sure word from God, for some unity-giving conception, for some dynamic that will lift men out of themselves and their sins and cynicism and give them faith and courage and hope.

Said a Hindu Nationalist to us as he was about to leave our Ashram after spending several weeks in our fellowship, "I go away without either faith or hope, but

I have found love here and that is something to hold to."
Amid the wreck of things he was grateful for anything
to which he could cling. After staying with us at a later
period he said as he went away, "I do not believe that
Jesus is the Truth or the Life, but I do think that he is
the Way, and that is something to begin on." In the confusion and yet in the utter sincerity of that Hindu Nationalist mind you find an epitome of the situation as it
confronts us in the mind of the modern man of the East.
You can see what that means for Christian opportunity.
It is simply overwhelming. When you have something
experimental, satisfying and saving in the midst of a
situation of that kind, the opportunity is too great for
words. Add to this the fact that the outcastes are feeling
their way into a completer life, and doing so on a very
wide scale, in fact on a scale of millions, and you have
the "open door" for which Christian missions has
prayed. Open door? It's off the hinges!

But at this very moment there has never been such a
deep opposition to Christian missions as now. The
Nationalist Hindu mentioned above said to me, "The
whole of the National Congress movement is opposed
to Christian missions." This is the more interesting in
view of the fact that the Christian movement a few years
ago seemed to have more in common with the National
Congress movement than any other body. There was an
inherent sense of inward understanding. Gandhi's ideas
of non-violent non-cooperation seemed to fit the Chris-

tian ethic and outlook and there was much inward kinship. One of the leaders of the movement said to me,
"It is you Christians who can understand our movement
better than any other for our ideas are inherently akin."
The cross seemed so vital in those days. Men went to jail
carrying New Testaments in their scant belongings, for
the New Testament spoke directly to their hearts
through their own movement. Gandhi and Christ had a
very close kinship in the mind of India in those days.
Then why has the Nationalist mind hardened against
Christian missions? That it has hardened there is no
doubt. Mr. Gandhi and the Nationalist press go out of
their way to find fault. I am not sure that this hardening
is against Christ as a person. He still grips the thinking
and the acting of many, perhaps of an increasing number even though they are outside of the Christian
church. But that there is a hardening against the Christian movement as such there is no doubt.

In looking for the reasons one need not dwell on the
fact that Christ has come to the East wrapped in the
habiliments of the West. He came handicapped from
the start. The West dominated the East. How can you
take a religion from the hands of your conquerors?
They may conquer your bodies, but will you allow them
to conquer your souls? In the area of religion there
could be the assertion of a soul-independence. The East
stiffened its inner being and held the sanctuary. "We
cannot give up our faith in our religion, it's the only

thing that we have left," said a Hindu youth to me. That handicap of being bound up with the conquering West has been and is still a real one, and will not be transcended till the East shakes off Western domination and stands free to choose her own faith within any inward inhibitions about the channel through which it comes. A free East will be free to choose.

But in addition to the general handicap of being brought by a conquering people, there is a local handicap to the Christian movement which has arisen in India through the coming in of the Reform Scheme in these recent years. The Reform Scheme which has just begun operation gives to India provincial self-government. The allotment of seats in the legislature and the filling of offices are on the basis of communal representation, that is, each religious community in India is given its share in the loaves and fishes of office according to the number of adherents. The assignment was made by the British government since these various communities could not come to an agreement. Religion was made the basis of representation.

All these provisions tighten up the whole situation between the communities. Numbers count. The future of the country will be determined by the community which can maintain and possibly add to its numbers. Conversion is the method of adding to the faith. Conversion then from one faith to another becomes at once something of national significance. It is no longer a religious question, it is now a political and cultural question. If the Moslems can convert in sufficiently large numbers, then they control India culturally and politically. The Hindus must maintain their numbers, there must be no falling away to any faith, in fact they must Hinduize the aboriginal tribes which have not been absorbed into the Hindu fold, and they must open the Hindu temples and its privileges to the outcastes, and above all they must stop conversion both to Islam and to Christianity, and they must try to reconvert those who have gone over to these other faiths. The Hindu is fighting for his cultural and political life. Christian missions have been caught in this jam of political influences.

Obviously, the thing for Christian missions to do was to lift the whole Christian movement out of this. It could do it by repudiating communalism, by saying that it would not stand politically for the Christian community but for the country. It could do this with very good conscience by pointing to China where there is no Christian community in addition to the Christian church. The Christians are Nationalists and are standing for the country and not merely for the Christian group. But in India there is a very definite Christian community in addition to the Christian church and the Christians were asked to take their part in the whole communal scheme of reforms. This was deadly in two ways. First, their influence and education really made them deserve more in the way of office and opportunity than their numbers would imply. Second, to get into that scheme of communalism cut straight across the Christianization of India. It would block it. Many Christian leaders pleaded that they renounce communalism, but the pressure was too great both from within the Christian community and from the framers of the scheme itself. The Christians have taken communal representation, at least for the time being. Some of us are still hoping that they may renounce it, lose their life in the country and find it again in moral and spiritual influence.

I have gone to the leaders of the country and have said to them this: A communalism has been built up around the Christian church, part of the fault is ours and part of it is yours. We segregated converts in the beginning, but you also helped in the formation of this community by your refusal to allow people to stay in their homes when they began to follow Christ. You threw them out and they were bound to form themselves into a separate communalism. If you are willing to allow people to stay in their homes and be frank, open Christians, members of a moral and spiritual organization, the Christian church, they need not change their dress, their names, their diet, and they may stand in the stream of India's culture and life. If you are willing to do this, then as far as we are concerned, we are willing to see the Christian community as a separate political entity fade out, leaving the Christian church as a moral and spiritual organization contributing its power to India's uplift and redemption.

Every single national leader to whom I have presented this matter has cordially agreed, jumped at it in fact. It has lifted the whole matter of conversion into a new plane; it has shed light on the vexed matter of conversion being mixed with political considerations. Mr. Gandhi's reply to my proposal was interesting, "If my son should become a Christian on the basis which you propose, namely that there should be no change of dress or of names and one could stand in the stream of India's life and culture and interpret his new faith, and if in his case there should be no liquor or tobacco involved, I should keep him in my home without penalty or disability." When I suggested to him that this was personal and asked him if he recommend this to India, he replied, "I would. And moreover if you will take this attitude, then most of the objections to Christianity would fade out of the mind of India."

This was important not only in regard to the immediate communal issue, but also in regard to the whole matter of conversion. Mr. Gandhi had taken an attitude of refusing to allow that conversion was legitimate under any circumstances; one should stay in his own faith. But in this statement he had conceded that it might take place. I think this was his inmost feeling in regard to the matter, but some months later he issued a statement which cancelled all that he had said to me. He found himself bound up with political considerations that made him back from that position, for it might give rise to the idea that conversion was now considered legitimate by him—legitimate in general, when he had only considered it legitimate under those particular circumstances. Apart from Mr. Gandhi there has been an eager acceptance of this position on the part of the national leaders whom I have consulted. It is the only position for us and for them to take. It saves us from further dividing the country with another communalism, it saves the Hindu from the loss of cultural and political power through conversion, and it saves religion from being the football of politics. But above all, it saves the Christian movement from being stultified at the central point, namely, the right to give its message and to win to its allegiance those who would take it.

Obviously the approach to the East must be simplified and clarified. We must cut away every extraneous issue and bring the matter down to where the issues are clear. To do this we must strip away from Christ and his message the things which have been built up around him. He must be presented to the East without complications. He must be the disentangled Christ.

At the close of an address the Hindu chairman said to the audience, "There have been certain stages in the approach of Christ to the soul of India. First he came to us and knocked at our doors in company with a trader. We looked out and we said within ourselves, We like you but we do not like your company. So we closed the door. Again he came, this time with a soldier on the one side and a diplomat on the other. Again we said within ourselves, We like you, but we do not like your company. And again we closed the door. Now he comes presented tonight standing in his right, entering into our lowly doors, the friend of the sick and the sinful; he is apart from everything but his own love and compassion. We say to this Christ, Enter, our hearts are yours." There is no doubt that this is the attitude of many.

While we must strip from Christ all that is extraneous we must also strip from our own hearts everything that hinders the presentation of that Christ. We cannot help but feel that we have a superior message, but if that sense of the superior creeps into us and makes us feel that *we* are superior, then we are unfitted to become the heralds of this message.

We must bring this message as a love offering to the people to whom we go. Infinite respect must be in our hearts for the people whom we approach. Their customs may be different, their habits may be obnoxious to us, but we must cultivate the sense of appreciation that would look past all this to the worth-whileness of the people and to the possibilities inherent in everyone. We must be tender and gentle in regard to any custom they may have. There is probably a reason for that custom. It may be that in the end it will have to go, but it may have to stay for it is rooted in a vital human need. We must believe that Christ came not to destroy, but to complete and to fulfill. We will therefore not be the enemies of the culture of any people, but be eager to preserve what is fine and noble in any race. We shall not try to make all alike, but out of the differences we shall make a richer harmony. Some Negro singers came to India and sang their wonderful spirituals in parts. A Hindu commenting on this said, "What a pity it was that they could not all sing the same tune." The Hindu sings in melody and the Negro in harmony and the Hindu wanted everyone to sing the same tune! How much richer we will be when there are differences and yet a central harmony amid these differences.

But in our approach to the East we shall not come with tentative attitudes to add confusion to the confusion of the East. We will not come dogmatically, but with a deep experimental certainty. The East wants to know what we know, not what we doubt. In arranging for a series of meetings in a city in the East the committee of arrangements wisely asked a non-Christian to become a member of the committee on arrangements. One of the Christian members suggested that they ask me to speak on some general subject, such as my travels, and then if the people were interested sufficiently and requested it, I should speak on religion. "No," said this non-Christian, "let him speak on some such subject as: 'What I believe and why I believe it.' " This is the attitude of the seeking East. They want to know whether we have a faith and why we have it.

Just now there came to me a youth, a graduate of a

great Moslem university, who was returning from a pil-
grimage to Mecca. When I asked him where all this
left him he replied, "Confused, and my faith is getting
dimmer." The Christian must come with an experimental certainty that rings clear and true amid the
surrounding uncertainty. A Nationalist Hindu said,
"I came to hear you for you seemed so cocksure
about everything and I was sure of nothing." I took
to heart the word "cocksure," for I did not want to
wear that word as a label. But inwardly I knew he was
wrong, for any certainty I had gained came through the
long hard way of experimentation and there were scars
on my faith. Christian missions must come with an experimental certainty amid a world of vast uncertainties.
Our approach must be sure.

If our approach is to be effective it must not merely
be verbal; it must be vital. We must let the people see
what we mean by the message. If we preach the kingdom of God then the people must see that kingdom in
demonstration. We must set up demonstration centers
of the kingdom—our homes, our schools, our *ashrams,*
our institutions must be cells of the kingdom. People
must see in operation the new principles and power in
the new society. It was said that the ancient world of
Greece and Rome was not won to the Christian faith
through the preaching of the message so much as by the
sight of the new society. Amid a world of decay this new
society, the fellowship, had vitality and reality. It gave

men courage and hope that there was the possibility of a renewal of the individual and of society on a large scale.

This brings me to the observation that the approach to the East must now be in a perspective that is larger than we have been used to. While the faith of the individual has been decaying in the East, the social and economic institutions have also been decaying. The pulsating East is wanting a method of reconstruction. Think of the demand that is laid on Christian missions by the very rise of a man like Jawaharlal Nehru with his passion for reconstruction. He is a left-wing socialist, sincere and honest and able. Talk to him about the necessity of having a personal faith and he is interested but not satisfied. He wants something that will go beyond that. Into that situation we must come with a message not less than the kingdom of God on earth. We must provide something that will remake the individual and the collective will, something so universal that it will take in the sum total of human relationships, and something so intimate that it will take in our own personal need. The kingdom of God gives just that. It is therefore the message that is so desperately needed at the present time in the East. Men will want us to compromise it and tone it down. We cannot.

A Hindu came to me and said, "We must get this message of the kingdom of God down to the very villages. It is the word that India is waiting for. But in order to do that call it '*Rama Rajya*,' the kingdom of

Rama. Then people will take it." We do want to accom-
modate to every national aspiration and demand we can.
But we cannot compromise. It is the kingdom of God,
and Rama and God cannot be equated. And it is the
kingdom of God as interpreted by Jesus and illustrated
and embodied in himself. In him the kingdom of God
meets the kingdom of this world and goes to the cross
at that meeting place. There this higher kingdom takes
on itself all the sin and sorrow and wrongness of the
lower kingdom to lift and save it. We must preach this
kingdom as a head-on and sweeping answer to the
world's need and we must do it without compromise,
for there is nothing else that can save the world except
just this.

Men will say they have the same things in their own
sacred books. The day I landed in India thirty years ago
I traveled to Lucknow from Bombay with a Moslem and
I began my missionary work at once—I read him the
Sermon on the Mount. When I was through and looked
up to see the effect it had on him his reply was, "We have
the same thing in the Koran." The defense was not that
it was not true, but that it was not new. But the kingdom
of God as interpreted by Jesus is new. While it gathers
up everything that is fine in the old it goes beyond this
fulfillment and presents something utterly undreamed of
—the God who would save us even if it means a cross to
him. We must preach this message then without the stam-
mering of the tongue or the hesitation of the heart.

DR. E. STANLEY JONES WITH TWO NATIONALIST LEADERS
WHO ARE WEARING THE GANDHI CAP

From "Heritage of Beauty"

ALL SAINTS' MEMORIAL CHURCH, PESHAWAR

II. THE MISSIONARY APPROACH TO THE WEST

There used to be a time when we pointed to the map and said that mission fields are here, they are there, and they were always not the country in which we as Christians lived. The "heathen" sections were shaded in black. We were white. That smug assumption has received a very severe blow. We know now that paganism is not something on the map—it is something in our hearts and that may be in both East and West. "The field is the world" and "the world" is not merely this geographical world, but the world of human relationships, the world of economic contacts, the world of the inner life. The field is all of life.

The missionary then has a double task in regard to the home base—he must help convert the whole of life there in general, and specifically he must help convert the church itself to the missionary idea and passion. For the church is not yet committed to it; individuals are, but the church as a church is hesitant and half-hearted in its missionary conception and passion. What then should be our approach to the church at the home base?

1. We do not ask you to support this movement through pity. That was in large measure the appeal when I came to the mission field thirty years ago. It was not good enough. True, there is enough to break your heart in human conditions in non-Christian lands, but these nations now are awake and sensitive and any ele-

ment of pity will be resented at once. Besides, this attitude creates in us superior attitudes as a "brother bounti-
ful" to inferior peoples. This is deadly to the missionary
heart. I do not mean that we should go at this in a
"hard-boiled" manner, either on the part of the missionary or those who sustain the movement at the home
base. There must be deep compassion underlying the
movement. But compassion and pity are different. Compassion suffers *with* another, its root meaning is just
that, but pity means that you bend over people in
order to do them good. "Mrs. Quality was a very grand
lady who liked to be kind to people not so grand as she
was, only they had to behave as if they realized that they
were not so grand as she was, or it did not do at all."
Missions must purge itself from all of that spirit to be
effective in this growingly sensitive age. I went to India
through pity, I stay through respect. I am proud to serve
a people with the culture and inheritance of my people
of India.

2. We think it is a fallacy to wait till you have solved
all the problems of the home base before you can support a missionary movement abroad. On that basis who
would do individual work for individuals anywhere?
For who feels that all his own problems are solved? Not
one of us! That we have hold of something very real
and something very saving we gratefully acknowledge,
but have we fully surrendered to it? Partially, yes. But
the complete abandon? Nevertheless, we feel that we

have a right to go to individuals with our message for
we have hold of something supremely worth while. If
we as individuals go to others with what we know to be
a saving message although all our own spiritual problems are not yet solved, then why should we not as a
nation send to other nations although we are deeply
conscious that we need the very gospel we are giving to
others? The test in the case of both the individual and
the nation is whether we are sincerely acknowledging
our own need and are trying to apply the message we
give to others to those needs. The fact is that if we
wait till all our problems are solved we shall never go
at all, for when this set of problems has been solved we
shall have a new set on our hands demanding solution.

Life is a growth and our problems grow with that
growth. If sending people to other lands meant the
blinding of ourselves to our own needs, then the missionary enterprise would not be legitimate. But the fact
of the matter is that the sending of missionaries to other
lands exposes our own needs. The missionaries returning
report what other people are saying about us; it makes
us search our hearts. Moreover, it is a very searching
thing to our own message when we expose it to the
conflict which presenting it to another people involves.
It means that our own message is purified in the very
presentation. Extraneous things have to be cut away and
only the really relevant things remain. I am persuaded
that Christian missions have done more to clarify Chris-

tianity at home than perhaps any other single force. The reaction upon Christian theology and practice at the home base has been one of the most beneficial things that has happened. Without this cleansing reaction it is quite probable that our Christianity would have degenerated. In saving others we have saved ourselves.

3. We would remind the home base that a faith that cannot be exported cannot be kept. If this faith does not belong to every man it belongs to no man. There is no such thing as a local truth. Truth by its very nature is universal. Two and two make four around the world. But two and two make five—that is local. Error by its nature is local. If therefore you take the attitude that your faith is good enough for you and the other man's is good enough for him, then what you mean is that neither one is universal and neither one is true. If therefore you find that you cannot share this faith with every man everywhere, you will soon find that you cannot keep it. It won't meet your need. For the human heart is one. Scratch down beneath the surface of outer differences, differences which have come largely through the difference in the social heredity, and you will find just a common humanity.

On a round world it is hard to tell where East ends and West begins. The fact is that our problems are no longer Eastern problems and Western problems—they are becoming just human problems. I find that when I move from one country into another the same problems confront men everywhere and the same message is valid everywhere. That is the glory of the Christian faith— there are no frontiers and there are no strange lands to it. A Moslem just interrupted me long enough to ask why it is that Moslems fear translating the Koran into languages other than the Arabic. Would it lose its power if they did so? Such a question does not arise with us. There is an inherent something in this message that is capable of going over into another language without loss of power and redemptive influence. Jesus Christ is the Son of man and as such he belongs to the sons of men. Should we try to confine him to our own land then we would have something other than Christ upon our hands. He would be localized, limited, untrue.

4. When we lose the power of propagation we are then in the process of decay and death. Life depends upon power to propagate life. When we lose the moral and spiritual offensive from our faith it is the beginning of the end. When they are dimmed our faith begins to dim with them. Christian missions is the test of the vitality of our faith.

5. This movement is not founded on a particular text of Scripture, although the Scripture is explicit about the universality of the Christian mission; but it is founded upon the very nature of the God revealed in Jesus Christ. The God whom we see in Jesus Christ loved the world, and so loved it that he gave his very heart, his own son. At the center of the Christian conception is the

mission idea and passion. To get rid of missions you would have to cut out the heart of God. The pulse beat of missions is in the very center of the universe. When Jesus said, "I must go on to the next towns," he was simply expressing what was inherent in the soul of God. The drive of redemption is founded in the love of God. If God is love then it cannot be abstract love, it must be concrete, vital, redemptive—and it must be universal, or it would not be love but snobbery. If the Christian is to be like God he cannot help but love in universal terms. The moment he tries to limit his love that love turns from love into racialism, the degeneration of love.

6. It is a truism and yet it is well to remind ourselves that all of Christianity at the home base is founded on the efforts of foreign missionaries. If we do not give ourselves to missions, then we must repudiate their gift to us. But if we did then we would have nothing left. For all we are we owe to Christian missions. There is not a liberty, an institution, a privilege, a single good thing in our civilization that is not blood-bought in a double sense, first by the blood of the Son of God and second by the blood of the missionaries who came and shared with our barbarous ancestors the message.

7. A world choice is now being made. We are straight up against the fact that this generation or at the most the next generation will have to decide between communism, fascism or the kingdom of God. The world

mind is being made up and these are the alternatives before us. We cannot stay where we are, for this old order is going to pieces under us. We need something to put under this toppling order. Which will it be: communism, fascism or the kingdom of God? The time of sifting has now come. We can no longer act as though we are neutral. We must be missionaries of something. If we stand where we are and do nothing then we are missionaries of decadence and chaos. We stand for the old and the old is decaying and going to pieces.

Do you want the world to go communist? Sit down and think what that means, what it means to the thing that you hold dear—your very faith. Do you want that to go? Do you want your universe to be a godless universe? Do you want the world to go fascist? That would not be godless, you say, for the fascists believe in religion. Do they believe in God? Hardly. Not when they make the state God. When the state is supreme, then where is the place for the supreme God?

Either one of these exacts too heavy a price for one's allegiance. We cannot take either one. And we cannot remain in the old. Then there is only one thing left: The kingdom! We do choose that. For it was Christ's choice and what he chose is supremely worth while. We cannot go astray following him. He has been right on every single issue so far. And now we come straight up to the question of whether we shall take his kingdom as the way out of our individual and collective chaos. And that question must be settled on a world scale. There are no localisms in it. Fascism is not local. Hitler says that there can never be peace in the world until there is one government, that one government of course, fascist! Is communism local? They say they cannot rest until the world has gone communist. Then does the Christian remain in petty localisms when these universal movements are pressing upon the heart and mind of the world for admittance? He must be universal or out of the game.

James Chalmers was killed and eaten by the savages of Papua. They found written in his Bible which his mother had given him these words opposite the story of Jesus standing on the shore, "Yes, Jesus stands on the shore of every country waiting for his missionaries." He does! But those shores now are not only geographical, they are the frontiers where the great issues of life are being decided: the economic, the social, the moral and the spiritual. He stands on those shores waiting for his missionaries. Does the church turn back to its devotions and leave him standing on those shores—alone? Or do we spring to his side and say, We are with you in life and death! THE KINGDOM—THE KINGDOM is our choice! We must do that and get everybody everywhere to do the same. In other words we must be missionary.

STATISTICS

CHRISTIAN MEDICAL WORK
IN INDIA, BURMA AND CEYLON

Hospitals	256
Dispensaries	250
Sanatoriums	10
Leper Homes	38
Medical Schools	3
Number of Hospital Beds	12,000
Number of Sanatorium Beds	755
Doctors, Foreign	350
Doctors, National	390
Nurses, Foreign	300
Nurses, National	900
Student Nurses	1,800
Operations, Major	44,000
Obstretrics, Total	32,000
In-Patients	285,000
Out-Patients	2,600,000
Total Current Expenses	Rs. 6,000,000

The Journal of the Christian Medical Association of India, Burma and Ceylon, May, 1937.

CHRISTIAN EDUCATION IN INDIA

	Institutions	*Students*
Elementary Schools	13,330	611,730
Secondary Schools	302	67,229
Colleges	31	11,162
Theological Colleges and Training Schools	25	556
Bible Training Schools	74	2,855
Teacher Training Schools	63	3,153

PERCENT OF LITERACY BY SEX AND RELIGION, 1931

Religion	All-India	Male	Female
All Religions	9.5	15.6	2.9
Hindu	8.4	14.4	2.1
Sikh	9.1	13.8	2.9
Muslim	6.4	10.7	1.5
Christian	27.9	35.2	20.3

Data from *The Statesman's Year-Book*, 1936, p. 129.

POPULATION BY RELIGION,[1] INDIA AND BURMA

	1921 Census	1931 Census
Hindu (Total)	216,734,586	239,195,140
Moslem	68,735,233	77,677,545
Buddhist	11,571,268	12,786,806
Sikh	3,238,803	4,335,771
Primitive Religions	9,774,611	8,280,347
Christian	4,754,064	6,296,763
Jain	1,178,596	1,252,105
Zoroastrian	101,778	109,752
Jews	21,778	24,141
Unreturned	......	2,879,438
Total	316,128,721	352,837,778

[1] Reprinted from *Directory of Christian Missions and Churches in India, Burma and Ceylon*, 1936-1937, p. 36.

CHRISTIANS—INDIA AND BURMA—ALL RACES AND SECTS

1891	2,284,380
1901	2,923,241
1911	3,876,203
1921	4,754,664
1931	6,296,763
1936	7,304,255 (Estimate)

Directory of Christian Missions and Churches in India, Burma and Ceylon, 1936-1937.

BIBLIOGRAPHY

General Description

COME WITH ME TO INDIA. Patricia Kendall. New York, Charles Scribner's Sons, 1931. $3.50.

INDIA LOOKS TO HER FUTURE. Oscar M. Buck. New York, Friendship Press, 1930. 50¢—paper 25¢.

INDIA REVEALS HERSELF. Basil Mathews. New York, Oxford University Press, 1937. $2.50.

THE LAND AND LIFE OF INDIA. Margaret Read. London, Edinburgh House Press, 1934. 2/—. (Available from Missionary Education Movement. 80¢.)

THE LEGACY OF INDIA. G. T. Garratt, editor. New York, Oxford University Press, 1937. $4.00.

MY INDIA. Lillian L. Ashby and Roger Whately. Boston, Little, Brown & Co., 1937. $3.00.

RENASCENT INDIA: FROM RAM MOHAN ROY TO MOHANDAS GANDHI. H. C. H. Zacharias. New York, E. P. Dutton Co., 1933. $3.25.

SPOTLIGHTS ON THE CULTURE OF INDIA. James Lowell Hypes. Washington, D. C., Daylion Co., 1937. $3.00.

A HISTORY OF MISSIONS IN INDIA. Julius Richter. New York, Fleming H. Revell Co., 1908. (Out of print, but available in libraries.)

History and Politics

JAWAHARLAL NEHRU: AN AUTOBIOGRAPHY; WITH MUSINGS ON RECENT EVENTS IN INDIA. Jawaharlal Nehru. London, John Lane, 1936. 15/—.

CAMBRIDGE SHORTER HISTORY OF INDIA. 3 Parts in 1. New York, Macmillan Co., 1934. $4.00.

INDIAN GODS AND KINGS; THE STORY OF A LIVING PAST. Emma Hawkridge. Boston, Houghton, Mifflin, 1935. $3.50.

INDIA'S NEW CONSTITUTION. J. P. Eddy and F. H. Lawton. New York, The Macmillan Co., 1935. $2.10.

MAHATMA GANDHI; HIS LIFE, WORK, AND INFLUENCE. J. R. Chitambar. Philadelphia, John C. Winston Co., 1933. $2.00.

NATIONHOOD FOR INDIA. J. S. M. Meston. New Haven, Connecticut, Yale University Press, 1933. $1.50.

OXFORD STUDENT'S HISTORY OF INDIA. 13th edition. Vincent A. Smith. New York, Oxford University Press, 1931. $1.35.

POLITICAL INDIA, 1832-1932: A CO-OPERATIVE SURVEY OF A CENTURY. Sir John G. Cumming, editor. New York, Oxford University Press, 1932. $1.50.

RISE AND FULFILMENT OF BRITISH RULE IN INDIA. Edward Thompson and G. T. Garratt. New York, Macmillan Co., 1934. $7.50.

Social and Economic Conditions

BEHIND MUD WALLS. Charlotte V. Wiser and William H. Wiser. New York, Richard R. Smith, 1930. $1.50. (Available from Harper & Brothers.)

CASTE AND RACE IN INDIA. G. S. Ghurye. New York, Alfred A. Knopf, 1932. $4.00.

THE CHRISTIAN MISSION IN RURAL INDIA. Kenyon L. Butterfield. New York, International Missionary Council, 1930. 80¢.

THE GOSPEL AND THE PLOW. Sam Higginbottom. New York, Macmillan Co., 1921. $1.00.

INDIA'S SOCIAL HERITAGE. L. S. S. O'Malley. New York, Oxford University Press, 1934. $2.00.

THE KEY OF PROGRESS: A SURVEY OF THE STATUS AND CONDITIONS OF WOMEN IN INDIA. A. R. Caton, editor. New York, Oxford University Press, 1930. $2.50.

POVERTY AND POPULATION IN INDIA. D. G. Karve. New York, Oxford University Press, 1936. $1.50.

UP FROM POVERTY IN RURAL INDIA. 3rd edition. D. Spencer Hatch. New York, Oxford University Press, 1936. $1.50.

WITHOUT THE PALE: THE LIFE STORY OF AN OUTCASTE. Margaret Sinclair Stevenson. New York, Oxford University Press, 1931. $1.25.

Indian Religions and Philosophy

INSIGHTS INTO MODERN HINDUISM. Hervey D. Griswold. New York, Henry Holt & Co., 1934. $2.00.

THE LIVING RELIGIONS OF THE INDIAN PEOPLE. Nicol Macnicol. London, Student Christian Movement Press, 1934. 10/6. (Available from Missionary Education Movement. $3.50.)

MODERN RELIGIOUS MOVEMENTS IN INDIA. J. N. Farquhar. New York, The Macmillan Co., 1924. $2.50.

THE HERITAGE OF INDIA. Kenneth J. Saunders. New York, The Macmillan Co., 1932. $1.75.

INDIAN THOUGHT AND ITS DEVELOPMENT. Albert Schweitzer. New York, Henry Holt & Co., 1936. $2.50.

Educational Work

CHRISTIAN EDUCATION IN INDIA. Sir George Anderson and Henry Whitehead. New York, Macmillan Co., 1932. $1.50.

CHRISTIAN EDUCATION IN THE VILLAGES OF INDIA. Alice B. Van Doren. Calcutta, Association Press Rs/2. Available through International Missionary Council, London.

INDIAN NATIONALISM AND THE CHRISTIAN COLLEGES. Paul J. Braisted. New York, Association Press, 1935, $2.00.

NEW SCHOOLS FOR YOUNG INDIA. William John McKee. Chapel Hill, North Carolina, University of North Carolina, 1930. $4.50.

THE CHRISTIAN COLLEGE IN INDIA. Report of the Commission on Christian Higher Education in India. New York, Oxford University Press, 1931. $2.00.

Medical Work

CAMEOS FROM PURULIA. L. Margaret Sharpe. London, Mission to Lepers, 1936. (Available from American Mission to Lepers. 35¢.)

RATS, PLAGUE AND RELIGION. John Spencer Carmen. Philadelphia, Judson Press, 1936. $1.25.

Christianity in India

BUILDERS OF THE INDIAN CHURCH; PRESENT PROBLEMS IN THE LIGHT OF THE PAST. Stephen Neill. London, Edinburgh House Press, 1934. 2/—. (Available from Missionary Education Movement. 80¢.)

THE FRONTIER PEOPLES OF INDIA: A Missionary Survey. Alexander McLeish. New York, World Dominion Press, 1931. $1.50.

ALL IN THE DAY'S WORK. Godfrey E. Phillips. New York, Missionary Education Movement, 1929. Boards, 50¢; paper, 25¢.

CHRISTIAN MASS MOVEMENTS IN INDIA. J. Waskom Pickett. New York, Abingdon Press, 1933. $2.00.

HERITAGE OF BEAUTY; PICTORIAL STUDIES OF MODERN CHURCH ARCHITECTURE IN ASIA AND AFRICA. Daniel J. Fleming. New York, Friendship Press, 1937. $1.50.

INDIA AND THE CHRISTIAN MOVEMENT. V. S. Azariah. Madras, Christian Literature Society of India, 1936. As. 8.

AN INDIAN APPROACH TO INDIA. Milton Stauffer, editor. New York, Missionary Education Movement, 1927. Cloth, 50¢; paper, 25¢.

THE UNTOUCHABLES' QUESTS: The Depressed Classes of India and Christianity. Godfrey Phillips. New York, Friendship Press, 1936. 75¢, paper 40¢.

Biography

CHILDREN OF THE LIGHT IN INDIA. Mrs. Arthur Parker. New York, Fleming H. Revell Co., 1930. $2.00.

SADHU SUNDAR SINGH. Charles F. Andrews. New York, Harper & Brothers, 1934. $1.00.

SUSIE SORABJI, CHRISTIAN-PARSEE EDUCATIONALIST OF WESTERN INDIA. Cornelia Sorabji. New York, Oxford University Press, 1932. $1.50.

MAHATMA GANDHI: HIS OWN STORY. C. F. Andrews, editor. New York, The Macmillan Co., 1930. $2.50.

MAHATMA GANDHI AT WORK: HIS OWN STORY CONTINUED. C. F. Andrews, editor. New York, The Macmillan Co., 1931. $2.50.

AN AMERICAN DOCTOR AT WORK IN INDIA. Sir William J. Wanless. New York, Fleming H. Revell Co., 1932. $1.50.

MEN OF THE OUTPOSTS. Herbert Welch. New York, Abingdon Press, 1937. $2.00. (Isabella Thoburn, Francis Xavier.)

SIR JAMES EWING. Robert E. Speer. New York, Fleming H. Revell Co., 1928. $2.75.

Magazine Articles
International Review of Missions

BETHLEHEM, A CHRISTIAN VILLAGE IN THE PUNJAB. Kamolini Sircar. April, 1936, p. 195-205.

AN EXPERIMENT IN RESEARCH AT AN INDIAN CHRISTIAN COLLEGE. H. L. Puxley. April, 1936, p. 206-215.

EVANGELISM AND VILLAGE CRAFTS. Frank Ryrie. July, 1936, p. 321-328.

EVANGELISM IN INDIA. J. Z. Hodge. October, 1935, p. 495-505.

THE FUTURE OF CHURCHES AND MISSIONS IN INDIA. H. Gulliford. July, 1937, p. 353-358.

THE KEY METHOD OF TEACHING ILLITERATES. Frank C. Laubach. April, 1936, p. 235-249.

A SURVEY OF THE YEAR 1937. William Paton and M. M. Underhill. January, 1938, p. —.

UPBUILDING THE CHURCH IN ASIA. George T. Scott. October, 1936, p. 526-535.

Missionary Review of the World

CHRISTIAN MASS MOVEMENTS IN INDIA. J. Waskom Pickett. April, 1936, p. 167-169.

THE EMANCIPATOR OF INDIAN OUTCASTES. L. O. Hartman. April, 1936, p. 170-171.

HOW EDUCATION HELPS INDIAN GIRLS. Charlotte C. Wyckoff. July, 1936, p. 353-355.

A TRIP TO VELLORE. June, 1932, p. 367-368.

WHAT CHRIST HAS DONE FOR UNTOUCHABLES. V. S. Azariah. March, 1937, p. 131-132.

WHAT INDIAN WOMANHOOD OWES TO CHRIST. Mrs. Mohini Das. September, 1936, p. 412-413.

INDEX

A
           PAGE

All-India Women's Conference
           33, 36
Ambedkar, Dr. Bhim Rao
       53, 66-73, 79
    differences with Gandhi   69
    renounced Hinduism   70, 71
Azariah, The Rt. Rev. V. S.   4

B

Bibliography   219-221
Bielby, Miss Elizabeth   104
Bombay   13-19
Brayne, F. L.   80, 97
British influence   20-21, 27

C

Carruthers, Lyman B., M.D.   4
Christian approach to India   196
Christian population, statistics of
            172, 218
Christian Unity desired   156-157
    movements towards   185-188
Church, the Christian
    in a city   163-164
    in a village   165-167, 174
    in civic life   180-181
    missionary work of   192-194
    organization of   174-178
    on the mission field   170
Church, The Indian defined
            170-171
Church of India, Burma and
    Ceylon   177-178
Church organizations federated
    South India United Church
            176-177
    United Church of Northern
    India   177
    Lutheran Churches   177
Clough, Dr. J. E.   58
Cochrane, Dr. R. G.   118
Colleges in India
     138, 141-146, 154-155
    why maintain?   159-162
    women's   138-146
Communal System   23, 199-201
Constitution, The new   27-29

D
           PAGE

Doctors, Indian Christian   127
    missionary   104-105, 109-110
    women   104-105
Dornakal   167, 193

E

Education, adult   85-88
    agricultural schools   90-92
    coeducation   146
    for women   138-146
    higher Christian   131-162
    pioneers in   132, 134
    religious   191
    see Colleges
Educational system, beginnings of
             133
Evangelistic work in hospitals   113

G

Gandhi, Mohandas Karamchand
   25-26, 29, 53, 64-65, 68-69, 202-203
George V, visit to India   13-15
George VI, coronation festivities
            15-19
Giving, Christian   166, 182-185
Group action among Untouchables
            58-59

H

Health standards   88-89, 114
Hinduism, responsible for
    untouchability?   53-55

J

Jones, E. Stanley   4, 153

K

Katpadi Institute   92
Karma, doctrine of   56

L

Laubach, Dr. Frank C. 82, 86-87
Leadership, Indian, in education
           136-137
    in church life 175-176, 178-180
Lepers   115-118
Liberals   30
Lindsay Commission   149-151

PAGE

Literacy, need of in villages 81-83
  statistics 181-182, 218

M

Marquis of Lothian 161-162
Mass Movements 58, 62-64
Medical training 123-126
Medical work 102-130
  government agencies 107-108
  hospitals 110-114
  maternity cases 112
  public health campaigns 120-121
  see Doctors
Missionary work, three stages of 167-169
Moga, school at 83
Mohan, story of 155-156
Montagu-Chelmsford Reforms 22-24
Moslems 31, 74, 200, 206, 213
Mott, Dr. J. R. 153, 188

N

Nationalities in India 15, 17-19
Nationalists 24-25
  attitude toward Christianity 180, 197-198
National Christian Council 178-180, 188, 192
National Congress 25-27
Nehru, Jawaharlal 29-30, 79, 207
Nursing profession 122-123

O

Oliver, Belle Choné. M.D. 3

P

Peaceful Picketing 35-36
Pickett, Bishop J. Waskom 3, 189
Poem, With Open Heart 12

R

Rajahs 28
Reddy, Dr. Muthulakshmi 56
Religions 172, 218
Rice, C. Herbert; Mrs. Mary C. 4
Roman Catholics 172-174
Rural India 75-101
  a village scene 75-77

PAGE

changes in 77-81
economic uplift 89-90, 92-94
health in 88
literacy, need of 81-83
schools in 83-85

S

Sangli movable school 91
Sarda Act 32-33
Scudder, Dr. Ida 120, 144
Scudder Memorial Hospital 102-103
Self-government 22-25
Simon Commission 24
Statistical tables 172, 181, 217-218
Student Christian Movement 157-158
Superstitions 98-99
Swain, Dr. Clara 37, 104
Syrian Christians 172-173

T

Tuberculosis 118-119

U

Untouchables 39, 42-74
  characteristics of 49-51
  effect of Christianity on 59-64, 73-74
  facing a choice 71-74
  group action among 58
  names for 43-44
  numbers and location 51-52
Untouchability 44
  occupations 47
  origins of 45-47

V

Van Doren, Alice B 3
Villages
  Indian Christian 94-96, 100
  proportion of inhabitants 167

W

Warner, Gertrude Leggett 3
Women's Colleges 138-146
Women doctors, see Medical work
Women, prominent Indian 32-39, 147-148
Women, rural 96-97